Kevin Zraly's

AMERICAN

WINE GUIDE

2008

*"Wine being among the earliest luxuries
in which we indulge ourselves, it is desirable
that it should be made here and we have every soil,
aspect and climate of the best wine countries."*

—THOMAS JEFFERSON

Kevin Zraly's
AMERICAN
WINE GUIDE
2008

Sterling Publishing Co., Inc.
NEW YORK

Dedication

To the pioneers of American wine making, the French, Italian, German, Spanish, Irish, Finnish, and all of the other immigrants who persevered first on the East Coast of the United States, then to the Midwest and onward to the West Coast and now to all the 50 states.

To all the wine writers who critiqued the wines in the early days helping to improve the quality to where it is today—world-class American wines.

A special note on writers Leon Adams (*Wines of America*), Frank Schoonmaker (*Frank Schoonmaker's Encyclopedia of Wine*), Andy Dias Blue (*American Wines*), and William Masse (*Wines of America*).

Library of Congress Cataloging-in-Publication Data Available

10 9 8 7 6 5 4 3 2 1

Published by Sterling Publishing Co., Inc.
387 Park Avenue South, New York, NY 10016
© 2007 by Kevin Zraly
Distributed in Canada by Sterling Publishing
c/o Canadian Manda Group, 165 Dufferin Street
Toronto, Ontario, Canada M6K 3H6
Distributed in the United Kingdom by GMC
Distribution Services
Castle Place, 166 High Street, Lewes, East Sussex,
England BN7 1XU
Distributed in Australia by Capricorn Link
(Australia) Pty. Ltd.
P.O. Box 704, Windsor, NSW 2756, Australia

Printed in China
All rights reserved

Sterling ISBN-13: 978-1-4027-4403-7
       ISBN-10: 1-4027-4403-X

For information about custom editions, special sales, premium and corporate purchases, please contact Sterling Special Sales Department at 800-805-5489 or specialsales@sterlingpub.com.

Acknowledgments

It was my honor and privilege to work again with Inez Ribustello, former beverage director at Windows on the World restaurant in New York City.

It is always a pleasure working with my longtime editor and advisor, Steve Topping. This edition gained two more editors, New England–based writer Becky Sue Epstein, and east coast editor Richard Leahy of Vineyard and Winery Management.

Thanks to Michelle Woodruff, the one who kept all the details together, compiling the many labels, winery information, and editing, between myself and Sterling Publishing; to Jim Trezise of the New York Wine & Grape Foundation; Bill Nelson of Wine America; Gladys Horiuchi of the California Wine Institute; Stephany Boettner of the Oregon Wine Center; Doug Caskey, Executive Director of the Colorado Wine Industry Development Board; *Wine Business Monthly;* and also the Washington Wine Commission.

From Sterling Publishing: Original design by Kevin Hanek; page layout for this edition by Nancy Field, with art direction for the current edition by Chrissy Kwasnik and cover by Elizabeth Mihaltse and Adam Weiss; editing and project management by Steve Magnuson, Rebecca Maines, and Christine Gonsalves, with copyeditors Melanie Gold and Paula Reedy.

Contents

Introduction

AMERICANS ARE DRINKING American wines! More than 75 percent of wines consumed in the United States are from this country. The most encouraging trend over the past few years is that Americans are drinking wine on a daily basis, not only for its reported health benefits, but simply because it tastes good and pairs so well with all kinds of foods. While there are plenty of books written on French, Italian, and Spanish wines, there are very few available on American wines; and there is no wine guide that encompasses the wines from all fifty states.

This edition of *Kevin Zraly's American Wine Guide* amasses the history, renaissance, facts, figures, and lore of American wine. It represents my attempt to cover an industry and products that are making a discernible mark not only on these shores but also worldwide—and most definitely has sparked a passion within me. My own career in wine spans more than thirty years, and in that time two of the most notable—and, to me, exciting—trends in the world of wine have been the remarkable rise in the quality of wines produced in America and wine consumption in America. These two trends, of course, keep reinforcing each other, so we can continue to expect great things from American winemakers.

Another significant development for American producers and consumers came in a May 2005 Supreme Court decision that overturned laws in New York and Michigan that allowed residents to order directly from in-state wineries but not from out-of-state vintners. In a 5–4 decision in *Granholm v. Heald*, the justices rejected the inconsistency of the New York and Michigan laws. For American wine, this could be the most notable ruling since Prohibition, and it goes right to the core of how the growth of American winemaking had previously been hindered. Outside of the "Big Four" states— California, New York, Washington, and Oregon— distribution has been the main obstacle to growth, especially for smaller wineries. With its ruling, the Supreme Court has thrown the matter back to the states to revamp their own laws to either allow inter-state wine purchases or scrap mail-order wine sales altogether. Within months, New York had done just that, enacting legislation to allow out-of-state wineries to ship to the state's consumers. I believe new wine distribution laws will greatly improve the availability of many wines from smaller, boutique wineries around the country.

American wine also has an enormous "fun factor." To me, studying and tasting the wines from around the country is truly exciting. It is a lesson in geography, history, agriculture, and the passion of grape growers and winemakers. But I am not just talking about wines from the four top wine-producing states. I get really thrilled finding undiscovered gems in Arizona, North Carolina, Idaho, and beyond. In fact, there are now wineries in each of the fifty states. When I began studying wine in 1970, two-thirds of the states had no wineries at all. There are now more than 3,600 wineries in the United States, with an estimated two hundred to three hundred opening every year.

In the United States, visiting wineries has become a major form of tourism. "Wine trails" have sprung up all across the United States in combination with other historical landmarks in those particular regions. Wine has definitely gone mainstream in America.

Searching for America

My own love affair with wine began in 1970 when, at the age of nineteen, I visited my first winery, Benmarl, in New York's Hudson Valley. That experience struck a nerve. I felt deeply connected to the earth, the grapes, the growers, and, of course, the wine. My soul was stirred; I knew after this first visit that I needed to learn more about wine, winemaking, and wine culture. I continued my early education by seeking out and visiting other wineries in New York State, beginning with wineries in the Hudson Valley and on to those in the Finger Lakes area. I made trip after trip, trekking from vineyard to vineyard.

But that wasn't enough. Each winery I visited provoked an urgent desire to see and learn more about wine. I had taken the first steps of what would become a lifelong journey. I began going to wine tastings as frequently as I could, sampling wines from all over the world. I studied grapes, learning each variety and its characteristics until I was able to identify most of the grapes used in the wines I tasted. And I became obsessive in my study of viticulture and wine tasting. The more I learned, the more I needed to know.

In the early 1970s the Finger Lakes district of New York and the North Coast of California were the only two regions in America producing quality wine. I will never forget reading, in 1972, the cover of *Time* magazine. The headline read AMERICAN WINE: THERE'S GOLD IN THEM THAR GRAPES, referring to the renaissance of California winemaking. So that summer (my twenty-first year) I took time off from college and hitchhiked west to California. I stayed for six months, visiting every major winery I'd heard of, tasting the wine and absorbing as much as I could about California wines and wine culture.

THE BEST-KNOWN WINERIES OF CALIFORNIA IN THE 1960s

Almaden
Beaulieu
Beringer
Concannon
Inglenook
Korbel
Krug
Martini
Paul Masson
Wente

On that trip I discovered that although some California winemakers were committed to producing fine wine, top quality American wine was still hard to come by. I found only a very few California wines worthy of comparison to the quality European wine I'd tasted. The best California wine was yet to come.

In 1974, after graduating from college, I traveled to Europe to tour the great vineyards of France, Spain, Italy, Germany, and Portugal. I was astounded by the extent to which each country possessed unique wine traditions, producing an impressive variety of superior-quality wines. What struck me most was the difference between the Old World and the New. European wine was like classical music: complex, yet soft and memorable, nurtured and matured over centuries of tradition. American wine, on the other hand, was like rock and roll: young, brash, and new, honoring no rules.

Top 10 states in number of wineries

California (1658)	Pennsylvania (99)
Washington (323)	Ohio (92)
Oregon (230)	Texas (89)
New York (210)	Michigan (73)
Virginia (101)	Missouri (66)

For the first time, 55 percent of all wineries are located outside of California.

A year after I returned from Europe, fortune smiled on me: I became the first cellar master at Windows on the World—the world-class restaurant atop the newly built World Trade Center in New York City. When we opened, our customers favored European wines, primarily French Bordeaux and Burgundy, which was fine with me. My time abroad had taught me how to taste, what to buy, and how long to age each. However, I was still drawn to American wine, so in the late 1970s, I arranged for a return visit to California. To my delight, this time I found, just as *Time* had predicted, that California winemakers were beginning to produce more and higher quality wines, some of which were comparable to the finest European offerings.

I came back to New York and immediately revised the wine list at Windows on the World. My original wine list had been 90 percent French. My new wine list favored American wine by a three-to-one margin. Our customers were cautious but adventurous enough to taste. Once they sampled and enjoyed the delicious Sonoma Chardonnays and Napa Valley Cabernet Sauvignons, they too became believers. By 1980, American consumers had begun to take California wine seriously. But California wasn't the only state producing good wine. Other states and regions, such as Oregon, Washington, and Long Island

(New York), were developing excellent vineyards and wineries as well. Word on the street quickly spread, and in culinary circles conversation often began with "Have you tried the Oregon Pinot Noir and Pinot Gris?" followed by "What about Washington State Cabernet Sauvignon and Long Island Merlot?"

Fast-forward to today. California still produces nine-tenths of all wine made in the United States, but New York, Oregon, and Washington State produce great wines as well. I can enjoy a meal accompanied by wines from Virginia, Pennsylvania, Texas, or any of the fifty states.

Americans have taken on a whole new appreciation for wines throughout the United States. New vineyards and wineries have helped them learn about the art of winemaking and provided the opportunity for them to observe grape growing in their own state. In short, Americans have been rediscovering wine over the last twenty years. In fact, we are now the third-largest wine-consuming nation in the world, with projections indicating that within the next five years the United States will be the top wine consumer worldwide!

Finally, our time has arrived. Thanks to the conviction and determination of American producers, the demands of American consumers, and the savvy of American wine writers, and in spite of the many obstacles that prevented more rapid progress, I can proudly say that many of the best wines in the world are produced in the United States. I can confidently say that for the first time in its history America is becoming well known as a wine-producing nation.

Grapes are now the sixth largest agricultural crop in the United States.

CHAPTER 1

Wine Basics

BEFORE DELVING INTO the vast territory of American wines there is some basic information to learn and review about wines and winemaking. Your wine experience, whether in a retail shop or a restaurant, should be easy and fun—not frustrating. The information that follows will help you build and reinforce the foundation of your wine knowledge. This essential material has been culled from the most commonly asked questions in my Windows on the World Wine Course. These basics, along with an adventurous spirit, are the only prerequisites for an exciting exploration into the world of American wine.

Building Blocks

Wine is the fermented juice of grapes (and other fruits). Fermentation is the process by which the grape juice turns into wine. The simple formula for fermentation is:

$$\text{Sugar} + \text{Yeast} = \text{Alcohol} + \text{Carbon Dioxide } (CO_2)$$

Sugar is naturally present in the ripe grape. Yeast also occurs naturally, as the white bloom on the grape skin. However, this natural yeast is not always used in today's winemaking. In many cases, laboratory strains of pure yeast have been isolated and added to the grapes, each strain contributing something unique to the style of the wine. The fermentation process begins when the grapes are crushed and ends when all of the sugar has been converted to alcohol or when the alcohol reaches about 15 percent, the level at which alcohol kills off the yeast. The carbon dioxide dissipates into the air, except in the case of Champagne and other sparkling wines, where this gas is retained through a special process.

Grape Varieties

The major wine grapes come from the species *Vitis vinifera*. Both European and American winemakers use *Vitis vinifera,* which includes many different varieties of grapes—both red and white—including Chardonnay, Sauvignon Blanc, and Riesling,Cabernet Sauvignon, Merlot, Pinot Noir, Zinfandel, and Syrah.

However, there are other species besides *vinifera* used for winemaking in the United States. *Vitis labrusca* (example: Concord and Catawba grapes) is grown widely in New York and other Eastern and Midwestern states. *Vitis riparia* and *Vitis rotundfolia* are grown in several wine regions of the United States.

Hybrids, which are crosses between *Vitis vinifera* and native American species, have also been planted in the United States, primarily along the East Coast. Hybrids have been grown especially in cooler climates in the United States, because of their winter hardiness. Examples include the white varietals of Seyval Blanc, Vidal Blanc, and Traminette. The red varietals include Chambourcin and Baco Noir.

Although there may be about a hundred different wine grape varieties planted around the world, for our purposes we will focus on a few of the most successful wine grapes in the United States. For white wines, Chardonnay, Sauvignon Blanc, and Riesling are the three major grape varieties. And for red wines, the major grape varieties include Cabernet Sauvignon, Merlot, Pinot Noir, Zinfandel, and Syrah. Concentrate on these grapes, and get to know the characteristics that allow wine drinkers to distinguish one from another as you begin your study of wine.

Grapes are agricultural products that require specific growing conditions. For example, most red grapes need a longer growing season than do white grapes, so red grapes are usually planted in warmer locations. Just as you wouldn't try to grow oranges in

New York, you wouldn't try to grow grapes at the North Pole. The areas with a reputation for fine wines have the right soil and favorable weather conditions for the variety of grape grown there. Proper drainage is also a requisite. Weather considerations include the growing season, the number of days of sunlight, the angle of the sun, average temperature, and rainfall. The right amount of sun ripens the grapes properly to give them the sugar/acid balance that makes the difference between fair, good, and great wines. Vines in the United States are planted during their dormant periods, usually the months of April or May. A vine doesn't usually produce grapes suitable for winemaking until the third year, but will then continue to produce good-quality grapes for forty years or more.

THE MOST IMPORTANT FACTORS IN WINEMAKING

Geographic location
Soil
Weather
Grape variety
Vinification: the actual winemaking process

Grapes are picked when they reach the proper sugar/acid ratio for the style of wine the vintner wants to produce. (Sugar concentration is measured as Brix.) Wine producers also look for phenolics and color as indicators of ripeness. Go to a vineyard in June and taste one of the small green grapes. Your mouth will pucker because the grape is so tart and acidic. Return to the same vineyard—even to that same vine—in September or October, and the grapes will taste sweet. All those months of sun have produced sugar (Brix) in the grape as a product of photosynthesis.

June
3% acid
0 Brix

July
2.3% acid
10 Brix

August
1.7% acid
15 Brix

Harvest
September
0.9% acid
22 Brix

The Brix scale is a measurement of percentage by weight of sugar at specified temperatures in a solution. It was developed in 1897 by Austrian scientist Adolf Brix.

Talk About the Weather

Weather can interfere with the quality of the harvest, as well as with its quantity. In the spring, as vines emerge from dormancy, a sudden frost may stop the flowering, thereby reducing the yields. Even a strong windstorm can affect the grapes adversely at this crucial time. Not enough rain, too much rain, or rain at the wrong time can also wreak havoc. Rain just before the harvest, like the record rainfall in the Northeast in October of 2005, will swell the grapes with water, diluting the juice and making thin, watery wines. Lack of rain, as in the drought period in California's North Coast counties in the late 1980s, will affect the balance of the wines from those years.

A severe drop in temperature may affect the vines even outside the growing season. For example, in New York State the winter of 2003–04 was one of the coldest in fifty years. The result was a major decrease in production, with some vineyards losing more than 50 percent of their crop for the 2004 vintage.

A number of countermeasures are available to the grower. Some of these measures are used while the grapes are on the vine; others are part of the winemaking process.

PROBLEM	RESULTS IN	SOLUTION
Frost	Reduced yield	Various frost protection methods: wind machines, sprinkler systems, and flaming heaters
Not enough sun	Unripe grapes	Chaptalization (the addition of sugar to the must—fresh grape juice—during fermentation)
Too much rain	Thin, watery wines	Move vineyard to a drier climate
Mildew	Rot	Spray with copper sulfate
Drought	Scorched grapes	Irrigate or pray for rain
Too much acid	Sour, tart wines	Deacidify
Too much alcohol	Change in the balance of the components	Dealcoholize
Phylloxera	Dead vines	Graft vines onto resistant rootstock

Phylloxera

Phylloxera, a grape louse, is one of the grapevine's worst enemies, because it eventually kills the entire plant. An epidemic infestation in the late 1800s came close to destroying all the vineyards of Europe and the United States. However, the roots of native American vines are immune to phylloxera. After this was discovered, all the *Vitis vinifera* vines were pulled up and grafted onto phylloxera-resistant American rootstocks.

In the early 1980s, phylloxera again became a problem in the vineyards of California. Vineyard owners were forced to replant their vines to the tune of $15,000 to $25,000 per acre, costing the California wine industry more than a billion dollars.

Wine Characteristics

Color: The color of wine comes primarily from the grape skins. Removing the skins immediately after picking means that none of their color is imparted to the wine, and the wine will be white. Most of the quality sparkling wines of California are made with a larger percentage of red grapes than white, yet most of these wines are white. (The same is true of most French Champagne.) California's White Zinfandel is made from red Zinfandel grapes.

Tannin: Tannin is a natural substance that comes from the skins, stems, and pips of the grapes, and also from the wooden barrels in which certain wines are aged. It acts as a preservative; without it, certain wines wouldn't continue to improve in the bottle. In young wines, tannin can be very astringent and make the wine taste bitter. Generally, red wines have more tannin than do whites, because red grapes are usually left to ferment on their skins. Red wine

What to consider when determining whether a wine can or will age well

1. The color and the grape:

Red wines, because of their tannin content, can generally age longer than whites. And certain red grapes, such as Cabernet Sauvignon, tend to have more tannin than, say, Pinot Noir, and age accordingly.

2. The vintage:

The better the weather conditions in a given year, the more likely the wines from that vintage will have a better balance of fruits, acids, and tannins, and therefore the potential to age longer.

3. Where the wine comes from:

Certain vineyards have optimum conditions for growing grapes, including such factors as the right soil quality, favorable weather, good drainage, and the slope of the land. All of this contributes to producing a great wine that will need time to age.

4. How the wine was made (vinification):

The longer the wine remains in contact with its skins during fermentation (maceration), the more it will have of the natural preservative tannin, which will help it age longer. Fermenting and/or aging in oak also increases tannin.

5. Wine storage conditions:

Even the best-made wines in the world will not age well if they are improperly stored. For long-term aging, the best storage conditions for wine are 55°F and 75 percent humidity.

grape skins also contain resveratrol, which studies have indicated may help prevent some cancers.

Acidity: All wine has a certain amount of acidity. Generally, white wines are more acidic than reds (although winemakers always strive for a balance of fruit and acid). An overly acidic wine is also described as tart or sour. Acidity is a very important component in the aging of wines.

Vintage and aging: The vintage indicates the year the grapes were harvested, so every year is a vintage year. A vintage chart reflects the weather conditions for various years: Better weather usually results in a better rating for the vintage.

It's a common misconception that all wines improve with age. In fact, more than 90 percent of all the wines made in the world are meant to be consumed within one year, and less than 1 percent of the world's wines are meant to be aged for more than five years. The best American Cabernet Sauvignon, Zinfandel, Syrah, or port are examples of wines that will age more than five years.

Wines change with age. Some get better, but most do not.

Wine Regulation

Each major wine-producing country has government-sponsored control agencies as well as laws that regulate all aspects of wine production and set certain minimum standards that must be observed. In France, these regulatory responsibilities fall under the umbrella of Appellation d'Origine Contrôlée (AOC); in Italy it's Denominazione di Origine Controllata (DOC). In the United States, wine regulation is overseen by the Alcohol and Tobacco Tax and Trade Bureau.

Tasting Wine

You can read all the books written on wine to become more knowledgeable on the subject, but it is in the tasting of wines that you truly enhance your understanding. Below are the necessary steps for tasting wine. Follow them with a glass of wine in hand!

Wine tasting can be broken down into five basic steps: Color, Swirl, Smell, Taste, and Savor.

Color

The best way to get an idea of the color of the wine is to hold the glass of wine in front of a white background, such as a napkin or tablecloth. The range of colors that you may see depends, of course, on whether you're tasting a white or red wine. The table opposite gives some descriptions of the colors for both, beginning with the youngest wines and moving to older wines.

Color tells you a lot about the wine. In the case of white wine, a darker (or richer) color may tell you the wine is older, because white wine gains color with age. Or it may indicate the wine was aged in wood, which also adds color. For red wine, a richer color may indicate a younger wine; red wines, when they age, tend to lose color. As a general rule, I say that if you can see through a red wine, it's ready to drink.

The color of both red and white wines is also influenced by the grape variety. For whites, Chardonnay usually gives a deeper color than does Sauvignon Blanc. For red wines, Cabernet Sauvignon is usually darker than, say, Pinot Noir.

When teaching about wine, I always begin by pouring a glass of wine and asking the class what

	WHITE WINE	RED WINE	
young	Pale yellow-green	Purple	young
	Straw yellow		
	Yellow-gold	Ruby	
old	Gold	Red	
	Old gold	Brick red	old
	Yellow-brown	Red-brown	
	Maderized		
very old	Brown	Brown	very old

color the wine is. It's not unusual to hear some describe the wine as pale yellow-green; others call it gold. Everyone begins with the same wine, but color perceptions vary. There are no right or wrong answers, because perception is subjective.

Swirl

Swirl wine in your glass to increase the flow of oxygen through the wine. Swirling releases the esters, ethers, and aldehydes that combine with oxygen to yield a wine's bouquet. In other words, swirling aerates the wine and releases more of the bouquet and aroma.

THE HUMAN ELEMENT OF SMELL AND TASTE

Bouquet is the total smell of the wine.

Aroma is the smell of the grapes.

The "nose" of a wine is a word that wine tasters use to describe the bouquet and aroma of the wine.

The average person has five thousand taste buds.

Other sensations of wine include numbing, tingling, drying, cooling, warmth, and coating.

Smell

Smell is the most important step in the tasting process. This whole activity should never have been called "wine tasting" in the first place—"wine smelling" would be much more accurate since 90 percent of taste is really smell! Humans perceive just four tastes—sweet, sour, bitter, and salty—but the average person can identify more than two thousand different scents, and wine alone has more than two hundred. Once you've swirled the wine and released the bouquet, smell the wine at least three times. You may find that the third smell gives you more information than the first smell.

Pinpointing the nose of the wine helps you to identify certain characteristics that are difficult to describe. Many people ask me to tell them what a particular wine smells like. I prefer not to use pretentious words, so I may answer by saying the wine smells like an oak-aged Chardonnay. However, this rarely satisfies most people. They want to know more. I respond by asking them to describe what steak and onions smell like, and they say, "Like steak and onions." See what I mean?

The best way to learn your own preferences for styles of wine is to "memorize" the smell of the individual grape varieties. For white, begin by trying to memorize the three major grape varieties: Chardonnay, Sauvignon Blanc, and Riesling. Keep smelling them, and smelling them, and smelling them until you can tell the difference distinctly in a blind test. For the reds it's a little more difficult, but you should still begin with the three major grape varieties: Pinot Noir, Merlot, and Cabernet Sauvignon. Once you memorize their unique smells and can distinguish and describe them without using flowery words, you'll understand what I'm talking about.

For my wine school, I have compiled a list of five hundred words commonly used to describe an individual wine's characteristics. Here is a small excerpt:

aftertaste	character	hard	seductive
aroma	chocolate	hot	short
astringent	corky	legs	soft
austere	delicate	light	stalky
baked/burnt	developed	maderized	sulfury
balanced	earthy	mature	tart
big/full/ heavy	finish	metallic	thin
bitter	flat	nose	tired
body	fresh	nutty	vanilla
bouquet	grapey	off	woody
bright	grassy	pétillant	yeasty
	green	rich	young

Personally, I like my wine bright, rich, mature, developed, seductive, and with nice legs!

You're also more likely to recognize some of the defects of a wine through your sense of smell.

Following is a list of some of the negative smells in wine:

SMELL	WHY
Vinegar	Too much acetic acid in wine
Sherry*	Oxidation
Dank, wet, moldy cellar smell	Wine absorbed the taste of a defective cork (referred to as "corked wine")
Sulfur** (burnt matches)	Too much sulfur dioxide

*Authentic Sherry, from Spain, is intentionally made through controlled oxidation.

**Sulfur dioxide is used in many ways in winemaking. It kills bacteria in wine, prevents unwanted fermentation, and acts as a preservative. Too much can cause a burning and itching sensation in your nose.

Taste and Sensations

To many people, tasting wine means taking a sip and swallowing immediately. Proper tasting, however, is done more slowly, with your taste buds. You have taste buds all over your mouth—on both sides, underneath, and on the tip of the tongue, extending to the back of the throat. Don't bypass all of those important taste buds by swallowing too quickly. When tasting wine, leave it in your mouth for three to five seconds before you swallow. This warms the wine to your body temperature and creates more smells, all of which will be sent through your nasal passages to your olfactory bulb.

When tasting wine, be aware of the most important sensations of taste and your personal thresholds to those tastes. Pay attention to where these sensations occur on your tongue and in your mouth. As I mentioned earlier, we perceive just four tastes: sweet, sour, bitter, and salty (but there's no salt in wine, so we're down to three). Bitterness in wine usually indicates high alcohol content and high tannin content. Sweetness occurs when wines have some residual sugar after fermentation. Sourness (sometimes described as "tart") indicates the amount of acidity in wine.

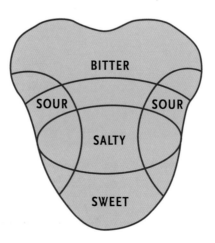

Sweetness: The highest threshold for sensing sweetness is located on the tip of the tongue. If there's any sweetness in a wine whatsoever, you'll get it right away.

Acidity: Acidity is sensed at the sides of the tongue, the cheek area, and the back of the throat. White wines and some lighter-style red wines usually contain a higher degree of perceived acidity than the more robust reds.

Bitterness: Bitterness is tasted on the back of the tongue.

Tannin: Tannin is not a taste but is a tactile sensation that begins in the middle of the tongue. As noted previously, tannin frequently exists in red wines or white wines aged in wood. When the wines are too young, tannin dries the palate too much. A lot of tannin in the wine can actually coat your entire mouth, blocking the flavor of the fruit. With age tannin softens, highlighting the fruit.

Fruit and varietal characteristics: These are not tastes, but smells. The fruitiness (the "body") will be felt in the middle of the tongue.

Aftertaste: Pay attention as the overall taste and balance of the components of the wine linger in your mouth. How long does the balance last? A long, pleasing aftertaste is usually a sign of a high-quality wine.

Savor

Once you've had a chance to taste the wine, sit back for a few moments and savor it. Think about what you just experienced, and ask yourself the following questions to help focus your impressions.

- Was the wine light-, medium-, or full-bodied?

- How was the acidity? Very little, just right, or too much?

- Is the tannin in the wine too strong or astringent?

- Does the tannin blend with the fruit or overpower it?

- What is the strongest component (sweetness, fruitiness, acidity, tannin)?

- How long did the balance of the components last (ten seconds, sixty seconds, longer)?

- Is the wine ready to drink? Or does it need more time to age? Or is it past its prime?

- What kind of food would you enjoy with the wine?

- To your taste, is the wine worth the price?

- This brings us to the most important point. The first thing you should consider after you've tasted a wine is whether or not you like it. Is it your style?

You can compare tasting wine to browsing in an art gallery. You wander from room to room looking at the paintings. Your first impression tells whether or not you like something. Once you decide you like a piece of art, you want to know more: Who was the artist? What is the history behind the work? How was it done? And so it is with wine. Usually, once *oenophiles* (wine aficionados) discover a wine that they like, they want to learn everything about it: the winemaker; the grapes; exactly where the vines were planted; the blend, if any; and the history behind the wine.

Most important, trust your own palate and do not let others dictate taste to you! The best definition of a good wine is one that you enjoy.

When is a wine ready to drink? This is one of the

most frequently asked questions in my wine school. The answer is very simple: when all components of the wine are in balance with your particular taste.

The 60-Second Wine Expert

I ask students in my wine course to spend one minute in silence after they swallow the wine. We use a "sixty-second wine expert" tasting sheet for them to record their impressions. The minute is divided into four sections: 0 to 15 seconds, 15 to 30 seconds, 30 to 45 seconds, and the final 45 to 60 seconds. Try this with your next glass of wine.

Please note that sometimes the first taste of wine is a shock to your taste buds, especally for wines with higher alcohol content, high acidity, and lots of tannin. The higher the alcohol, acidity, or tannin, the greater the shock. For the first wine in any tasting, it is best to take a sip and swirl the wine around in your mouth. Don't evaluate it. Wait another thirty seconds and take another sip, then begin the sixty-second wine expert evaluation.

0 to 15 seconds: If there is any residual sugar/sweetness in the wine, you will experience it now. If there is no sweetness in the wine, acidity is usually strongest in the first fifteen seconds. Look for the fruitiness of the wine and how it is balanced with the acidity or sweetness. What is the strongest component?

15 to 30 seconds: After sweetness or acidity, look for great fruit sensation. After all, that is what you're paying for! By the time you reach thirty seconds, you should experience a nice balance of all the components. By this time, you can identify the weight of the wine. Is it light-, medium-, or full-bodied? Start to think about what kind of food you can pair with this wine.

30 to 45 seconds: At this point you can begin to formulate an opinion of the wine, whether you like it or not. Not all wines need sixty seconds of thought. Lighter-style wines, such as Riesling, Pinot Grigio, and Seyval Blanc, will usually show their best at this point, and the fruitiness, acidity, and sweetness of a great Riesling should be in perfect harmony. For quality red and white wines, acidity—which is a very strong component (especially during the first thirty seconds)—should be in balance with the fruit of the wine.

45 to 60 seconds: Very often wine writers use the term "length" to describe how long the components, balance, and flavor continue in the mouth. Concentrate on the length of the wine in these last fifteen seconds. In big, full-bodied red wines such as the Syrahs, Merlots, Zinfandels, Cabernets, and even some full-bodied Chardonnays, concentrate on the level of tannin in the wine. Just as the acidity and fruit balance are major concerns in the first thirty seconds, it is now the tannin and fruit balance you are looking for in the last thirty seconds. If the fruit, tannin, and acid are all in balance at sixty seconds, the wine is probably ready to drink. Does the tannin overpower the fruit? If it does by the sixty-second mark, I will then begin to question whether I should drink the wine now or put it away for more aging.

It is extremely important to me that if you want to learn the true taste of the wine, you take *at least* one minute to concentrate on all of its components. In my classes it is reassuring to see more than a hundred students silently taking one minute to analyze a wine. Some close their eyes, some bow their heads in deep thought, others write notes.

One final point: Sixty seconds to me is the minimum time to wait before making a decision about a wine. Many great wines continue to show balance well past 120 seconds. The best wine I ever tasted lasted more than three minutes—that's three minutes of perfect balance of all components!

HOW TO TASTE WINE

Step One: Look at the color of the wine.
Step Two: Smell the wine three times.
Step Three: Put the wine in your mouth and leave it there for three to five seconds.
Step Four: Swallow the wine.
Step Five: Wait and concentrate on the wine for sixty seconds before discussing it.

CHAPTER 2

American Wine: A History

AMERICANS ARE NOW drinking more wine than ever before. In 2006, Americans consumed three gallons of wine per person, and sales topped $22 billion. A Gallup Poll released in 2005 showed that, for the first time in the poll's sixty-year history, wine drinkers outnumbered beer drinkers in the United States. Fueled by an 18 percent increase in wine drinking by Americans, 39 percent of drinkers say they drink wine most often, compared with 36 percent who say they choose beer. How dramatic are these figures? Well, in 1992, U.S. drinkers preferred beer 47 percent to 27 percent. The growth in wine production has been similarly strong. In 1975, the United States supported 580 wineries, a number that has grown to more than 3,600 today. For the first time in American history, all fifty states produce wine.

California is by far the leading wine-consuming state in the United States, with more than 42 million cases of wine sold each year. New York is a distant second, with 19 million cases sold. The next five states, ranked in order of wine consumption, are Florida, Texas, Illinois, New Jersey, and Pennsylvania.

Within the United States, California produces 90 percent of domestic wine, with Washington, New York, and Oregon producing an additional 8 percent.

Before looking at specific American wines and wineries, it's important to know a bit about the history of winemaking in the United States. While we often think of the wine industry as "young" in America, its roots go back some four hundred years.

THE TOP FIVE WINE-PRODUCING COUNTRIES IN THE WORLD

RANK	COUNTRY
1	France
2	Italy
3	**United States**
4	Spain
5	Argentina

THE TOP FIVE WINE-CONSUMING COUNTRIES IN THE WORLD

RANK	COUNTRY
1	France
2	Italy
3	**United States**
4	Germany
5	Spain

THE WORLD'S TOP PER CAPITA WINE-CONSUMING COUNTRIES

RANK	COUNTRY	GALLONS/PERSON
1	Luxembourg	16.0
2	France	15.8
3	Italy	14.3
4	Portugal	13.0
5	Croatia	12.4
33	**United States**	3.0

William Penn planted the first Pennsylvania vineyard in 1683.

Winemaking in the United States: The Early Years

The Pilgrims and early pioneers paved the way for American wine. Upon arriving in America, the early settlers, accustomed to drinking wine with meals, were delighted to find grapevines growing wild. These thrifty, self-reliant colonists thought they had found in this species (*Vitis labrusca,* primarily) a means of producing their own wine, which would end their dependence on the costly import of wine from Europe.

The early settlers cultivated the local grapevines, harvested the grapes, and made their first American wine. The taste of the new vintage was disappointing, however; wine made from New World grapes possessed an unfamiliar and entirely different flavor than wine made from European grapes. Undaunted, they ordered cuttings from Europe of the *Vitis vinifera* vine, which had for centuries produced the finest wines in the world. When the cuttings arrived by ship, the colonists, having paid scarce, hard-earned money for these new vines, planted and tended them with great care. They were eager to taste their first New World wine made from European *vinifera* grapes.

Vitis labrusca, the "slip-skinned" grape, is native to both the Northeast and the Midwest and produces a unique flavor. It is used in making grape juice—the bottled kind you'll find on supermarket shelves (think Welch's). Wine produced from *labrusca* grapes tastes, well, more "grapey" than European wines.

The three major types of wine produced in the United States are made from the following species of grapes:

NATIVE AMERICAN:

Vitis labrusca, such as the Concord, Catawba, and Niagara grapes; *Vitis rotundifolia* (commonly called Scuppernong); and *Vitis riparia.*

EUROPEAN:

Vitis vinifera, such as Riesling, Pinot Grigio, Sauvignon Blanc, Chardonnay, Pinot Noir, Merlot, Cabernet Sauvignon, Zinfandel, and Syrah.

HYBRIDS:

A cross between two species, for example vinifera and labrusca, to produce such grapes as Seyval Blanc, Vidal Blanc, Baco Noir, Traminette, and Chambourcin.

Unfortunately, despite careful cultivation, few of the European vines thrived. Many died, and those that did survive produced few grapes, which yielded very poor quality wine. Early settlers blamed the cold climate, but today we know that their European vines also lacked immunity to the New World's plant diseases and pests. If the colonists had had access to modern methods of pest and disease control, the *Vitis vinifera* grapes would have thrived then, just as they do today. However, for the next two hundred years every attempt at establishing varieties of *vinifera*—either intact or through crossbreeding with native vines—failed. Left with no choice, growers throughout the Northeast and Midwest returned to planting *Vitis labrusca,* North America's vine, and a small wine industry managed to survive.

The French Huguenots established colonies in Jacksonville, Florida, in 1562 and produced wine using the wild Scuppernong grape, a variety of the most common North American grape, *Vitis rotundifolia*. Evidence indicates that there was a flourishing wine industry in 1609 at the site of the early Jamestown settlements. In 2004 an old wine cellar was discovered in Jamestown with an empty wine bottle dating back to the seventeenth century.

Americans never really got used to the taste of this wine, however, and European wine remained the preferred—though high-priced—choice. The failures of these early attempts to establish a wine industry in the United States, along with the high cost of imported wines, resulted in decreased demand for wine. Gradually, American tastes changed and wine served at mealtime was reserved for special occasions; beer and whiskey gradually supplanted wine's traditional place in American homes.

American Winemaking Goes West

Wine production in the West began with the Spanish. As Spanish settlers began pushing northward from Mexico, the Catholic Church followed, and the era of mission building began.

Early missions were more than just churches: They were entire communities conceived as self-sufficient fortifications protecting Spanish colonial interests throughout the Southwest and along the Pacific Coast. Besides growing their own food and making their own clothing, these early settlers also made their own wine, produced primarily for use in the Church, as sacramental wine was important in Church ritual. (Perhaps higher-quality wine was an important factor in attracting congregants!) The demand for wine led Padre Junípero Serra to bring *Vitis vinifera* vines— brought to Mexico by the Spaniards—from Mexico to California in 1769. These vines took root, thriving in California's moderate climate and forming the foundation of the first true California wine industry, albeit on a small scale. The early missionaries set up wineries in parts of Southern California, planting a grape variety known as the Mission Grape. Unfortunately, it did not have the potential to produce great wine. The first commercial winery was located in the area we know today as Los Angeles.

The Other Gold: The California Grapevine

Two events occurred in the mid-1800s that resulted in an explosive growth of quality wine production. The first was the 1849 California Gold Rush. With a huge surge of immigrants pushing steadily westward, California's population exploded. Along with their hopes of finding treasure, immigrants from Europe and the East Coast brought their winemaking traditions. Unsuccessful in finding gold nuggets, many discovered a different kind of gold: California's grapevines. They cultivated the *vinifera* vines planted by the early Spanish settlers and were soon producing good-quality commercial wine, although in small quantities.

The second critical event occurred in 1861, when the governor of California, understanding the importance of viticulture to the state's growing economy, commissioned Count Agoston Haraszthy to select and import classic *Vitis vinifera* cuttings—such as Riesling, Zinfandel, Cabernet Sauvignon, and Chardonnay—from Europe. The count traveled to Europe, returning with more than a hundred thousand carefully selected vines. Due to the climatic conditions in California, these grape varieties not only thrived, they produced good-quality wine. Serious California winemaking began in earnest. During this period the Civil War broke out in the United States, leaving the fledgling wine industry with very little government attention or support. Nevertheless, the quality of California wine improved dramatically over the next thirty years.

Booming Market Demand

In 1863, while California wines were flourishing, European vineyards were in trouble. Phylloxera—an aphid pest native to the American East Coast that is very destructive to grape crops—began attacking European vineyards. While American native *Vitis labrusca* is resistant to phylloxera, Europe's *Vitis vinifera* is not. The infestation arrived in Europe on cuttings from native American vines exported for experimental purposes; it proved devastating. Over the next two decades, the phylloxera blight destroyed tens of thousands of acres of European vines, severely diminishing European wine production just as demand was rapidly growing.

At this time California was virtually the only region in the world producing wine made from European grapes, and demand for its wines skyrocketed. This helped develop, almost overnight, two huge markets for California wine. The first market clamored for good, inexpensive yet drinkable wine produced on a mass scale. The second market sought higher-quality wines.

California growers responded quickly to both demands, and by 1876 California was producing more than 2.3 million gallons of wine per year, some of very high quality. California was, for the moment, the new center of global winemaking. Unfortunately, in that same year, phylloxera arrived in California and began attacking its vineyards. Once phylloxera arrived, it spread as rapidly as it had in Europe, leaving the same kind of devastation. The California wine industry faced financial ruin. To this day, the phylloxera blight remains the world's most destructive crop epidemic ever recorded.

Luckily, other states had continued producing wine made from *labrusca* vines, and American wine production didn't grind to a complete halt. By the late 1800s, California, New York, Ohio, and Missouri had become the major wine-producing states.

Honeymooning in the Napa Valley in 1880, Robert Louis Stevenson described the efforts of local vintners to match soil and climate with the best possible varietals. "One corner of land after another...this is a failure, that is better, this is best. So bit by bit, they grope about for their Clos de Vougeot and Lafite...and the wine is bottled poetry."

Shortly after the blight reached California, years of research by European winemakers yielded a defense against the pernicious phylloxera aphid, by successfully grafting *Vitis vinifera* vines onto the rootstock of native American species (which were immune to the phylloxera). These new hybrids combined the hardy disease-resistant rootstock of the native American *labrusca* with the variety and quality of Europe's *Vitis vinifera,* rescuing the European wine industry.

Americans followed, and the California wine industry not only recovered but flourished, producing better quality wines than ever before. In 1899 and 1900, American wines won medals in international competitions, gaining the respect and admiration of the world. Forty different American wineries won medals at the 1900 Paris Exposition, including wines from California, New Jersey, New York, Ohio, and Virginia. And it only took three hundred years!

Prohibition: Yet Another Setback

In 1920, the Eighteenth Amendment to the United States Constitution was enacted, creating yet another serious setback to the American wine industry. The National Prohibition Act, also known as the Volstead Act, prohibited the manufacture, sale, transportation, importation, exportation, delivery, or possession of intoxicating liquors for beverage purposes, and nearly destroyed what had become a thriving national industry. In 1920 there were more than seven hundred wineries in California. By the end of Prohibition there were 160.

If Prohibition had lasted only four or five years, its impact on the wine industry might have been negligible. But it continued for thirteen years, during which time grapes went underground literally and figuratively, becoming an important commodity in the criminal economy. One loophole in the Volstead Act allowed for the manufacture and sale of sacramental wines, medicinal wines for sale by pharmacists with a doctor's prescription, and medicinal wine tonics (fortified wines) sold without prescription. Perhaps more important, Prohibition allowed anyone to produce up to two hundred gallons of fruit juice or cider each year. The fruit juice, which was sometimes made into concentrate, was ideal for making wine. Some of this yield found its way to bootleggers throughout America who did just that. But not for long, because the government stepped in and banned the sale of grape juice, preventing illegal wine production. Vineyards stopped being planted, and the American wine industry ground to a halt.

One way to get around Prohibition...

During Prohibition, people would buy grape concentrate from California and have it shipped to the East Coast. The top of the container was stamped in big, bold letters:

Caution:
Do not add sugar or yeast or else
fermentation will take place!

Of course, we know the formula:

Sugar + Yeast = Alcohol + Carbon Dioxide (CO_2)

Do you want to guess how many people had the sugar and yeast ready the very moment the concentrate arrived?

Prohibition produced the Roaring Twenties and fostered more beer and distilled-spirit drinkers than wine drinkers, because the raw materials were easier to come by. But fortified wine, or medicinal wine tonic—containing about 20 percent alcohol, which made it more like a distilled spirit than regular wine—was still available and became America's number one wine. Thunderbird and Wild Irish Rose, to name two examples, are fortified wines. American wine was soon popular more for its effect than its taste; in fact, the word *wino* came into use during the Depression to describe those unfortunate souls who turned to fortified wine to forget their troubles.

Prohibition was repealed in 1933, but its impact would be felt for decades. During Prohibition, thousands of acres of valuable grapes around the country had been plowed under. Even after winemaking was decriminalized, wineries nationwide continued to shut down and the industry dwindled to a handful of survivors, mostly in California and New York, as Americans had lost interest in quality wine. Many growers on the East Coast returned to producing grape juice—the ideal use for the American *labrusca* grape.

The federal government, in repealing Prohibition, empowered states to legislate the sale and transportation of alcohol. Some states handed control to counties and, occasionally, municipalities—a tradition that continues today, varying from state to state and often from county to county.

Hard Times for Wine: 1933–68

Although Prohibition was devastating to the majority of American wine producers, some survived by making sacramental wines. Beringer, Beaulieu, and the Christian Brothers are three wineries that weathered this dry time. Since these wineries didn't have to interrupt production during Prohibition, they had a jump on those that had to begin again from scratch in 1933.

From 1933 to 1968, grape growers and winemakers had little more than personal incentive to produce quality wine. Many made inexpensive, nondescript, and mass-produced wines. These were commonly called jug wines, named for the containers in which they were bottled. The best-selling wineries during these years were Almaden, Gallo, and Paul Masson. A few wineries, notably in California, were producing some good wines, but the majority of American wines in this period were ordinary.

SOME OF THE DILEMMAS FACING WINEMAKERS AFTER PROHIBITION

- Locate on the East Coast or the West Coast?
- Make sweet wine or dry wine?
- Make high-alcohol wine or low-alcohol wine?
- Make inexpensive bulk wine or premium wine?

The Reawakening of American Wine

It is difficult to pinpoint exactly when the American wine renaissance began, but let's start in 1968, when, for the first time since Prohibition, table wines—wines with alcohol content between 7 and 14 percent—outsold fortified wines. Although American wines were improving, consumers still believed the best wines were made in Europe, especially France.

In the mid-'60s and early '70s, a small group of dedicated winemakers, determined that California could produce wines equal to the finest of France, began concentrating on making high-quality wine. Their early wines, though not world class, demonstrated potential and began attracting the attention of astute wine writers and wine enthusiasts around the country.

As their product continued to improve, these winemakers began to realize that to market their wine successfully they needed a way to differentiate their quality wines from California's mass-produced wines—with generic names such as Burgundy, Chablis, or Chianti—and to ally their wines, at least in the minds of wine buyers and consumers, with European wines. Their brilliant strategy was to label their best wines by varietal.

Varietal designation calls the wine by the name of the predominant grape used to produce it: Chardonnay, Cabernet Sauvignon, Pinot Noir, etc. Savvy consumers learned quickly that a wine labeled Chardonnay would have the general characteristics of any wine made from that grape. This made wine buying easier for both wine buyers and sellers.

Varietal labeling spread rapidly throughout the industry and became so successful that, in the 1980s, varietal designation became an American industry standard. The result: The federal government increased the requirement for varietal content from 51 percent to 75 percent.

Today, varietal labeling is the norm for the highest quality American wines. It has been adopted by many other countries, and has helped bring worldwide attention to California wine. California's success inspired winemakers in other regions of the United States to refocus on producing high-quality wine.

American Wine Appreciation

Buying American wine intelligently means having knowledge about and familiarity with each wine-producing state, as well as the regions within the state. Some states—or even regions within a state—may specialize in white wine, others in red, and, going further, there are even regions that specialize in wine made using a specific grape variety. Therefore, it is helpful to know the defined grape-growing areas within each state or region, called American Viticultural Areas (AVAs).

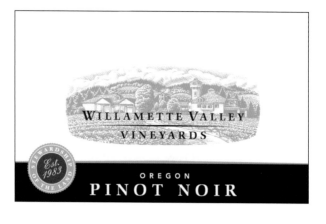

American Viticultural Areas

AVAs, specific grape-growing areas distinguishable by geographical features with delineated boundaries within a state or a region, are recognized by and registered with the federal government. AVA designation began in the 1980s and is styled after the European regional system. In France, Bordeaux and Burgundy are strictly enforced regional appellations (marked *Appellation d'Origine Contrôlée,* or AOC); in Italy, Tuscany and Piedmont are recognized as zones (marked *Denominazione di Origine Controllata,* or

DOC). The Napa Valley, for example, is a defined viticultural area in the state of California. Yakima Valley
is an AVA located in Washington State; both Oregon's
Willamette Valley and New York's Finger Lakes
districts are similarly identified.

There are about 175 viticultural areas in the United
States (see map in back flap, and individual state
maps in chapter 4), more than a hundred of which are
located in California. The AVA concept is important to
wine buying and will continue to be so as individual
AVAs become known for certain grape varieties or
wine styles. If an AVA is listed on the label, at least 85
percent of the grapes must come from that region.

Vintners are discovering, as their European coun-
terparts did years ago, which grapes grow best in
which particular soils and climatic conditions. For
example, the Napa Valley, which is probably the best-
known AVA in the United States, is renowned for its
Cabernet Sauvignon. Within Napa, there is a smaller
inner district called Carneros, which has a cooler climate. Since Chardonnay and Pinot Noir need a
cooler growing season to mature properly, these
grape varieties are especially suited to that AVA. In
New York, the Finger Lakes region is noted for Riesling. And those of you who have seen the movie

Sideways know that Santa Barbara is another great place for Pinot Noir.

Although not necessarily a guarantee of quality, an AVA designation identifies a specific area well known and established for its wine. It is a point of reference for winemakers and consumers. A wine can be better understood by its provenance, or where it came from. The more knowledge you have about a wine's origin, by region and grape, the easier it is to buy even unknown brands with confidence.

Choosing American Wine

The essence of this book is to simplify American wine for those who are buying (or selling) it. Do you prefer lighter or heavier wines; red wine or white; sweet wine or dry? To begin, you must learn the general characteristics of the major red and white grapes. Understanding these fundamental differences makes selecting an appropriate wine less difficult, as they help define the wine's style—and

EST. 1969

CUVAISON

PINOT NOIR
NAPA VALLEY
Carneros

ALC. 14.5 % BY VOL.

selecting the style of wine you want is the first decision you'll need to make.

Next, determine your price range. Are you looking for a nice, everyday wine for under ten dollars?
Or are you in the market for a twenty-five- or one-
hundred-dollar wine? Set your limit and stick to it.
You'll find the style of wine you're looking for at
almost any price.

Finally, learn how to read the label (see page 182).
Some of the highest quality wines in the United
States come from individual vineyards. The general
rule is: The more specific the label, the better the
quality of wine. All the important information about
any American wine appears on the label. Since the
federal government controls wine labeling and has
established standards, all American wine labels,
regardless of where in the United States the wine was
produced, contain essential information that con-
forms to national standards. This standardization
can assist you in making informed decisions about
the wine you're about to purchase or pour.

Dominus

Napa Valley

2001

Christian Moueix

ALC.14.1% BY VOL.-750 ML

NAPA VALLEY RED WINE
CONTAINS SULFITES - PRODUCED AND BOTTLED BY
DOMINUS ESTATE, YOUNTVILLE, CALIFORNIA, U.S.A.

Proprietary Wines

The most recent worldwide trend is to ignore all existing standards by giving the highest quality wines a proprietary name. A proprietary name helps high-end wineries differentiate their best wines from other wines from the same AVA, from similar varietals, and even from their own other offerings. In the United States, many of these proprietary wines fall under the category called Meritage (see page 208). Some examples of American proprietary wines are Dominus, Opus One, and Rubicon.

Federal laws governing standards and labels are another reason select wineries are increasingly using proprietary names. Federal law mandates, for example, that if a label lists a varietal, at least 75 percent of the grapes used to make the wine must be of that varietal.

Imagine a talented, innovative winemaker in the Walla Walla region of Washington State. This winemaker is determined to produce an outstanding,

WOODWARD CANYON

Walla Walla Valley
Estate Red Wine

ALC. 13.9% BY VOL.

full-bodied Bordeaux-style wine consisting of 60 percent Cabernet Sauvignon blended with several other grapes. Our ambitious winemaker has used his best soil for the vines, nurturing them with care and love. He has invested considerable time and labor to produce a really great wine: a wine suitable for aging that will be ready to drink in five years, but will be even better in ten.

After five years, our winemaker tastes the fruits of his labor and voilà! It is delicious, with all the promise of a truly outstanding wine. But how does he distinguish this wine; how can he attract buyers willing to pay a premium price for an unknown wine? He can't label it Cabernet Sauvignon, because less than 75 percent of the grapes are of that type. For this reason, many producers of fine wines are beginning to use proprietary names. It's indicative of the healthy state of the American wine industry as well. More and more winemakers are turning out better and better wines, and the very best is yet to come!

CHAPTER 3

Wine Shopping in the U.S.A.

TODAY'S WINE BUYER has thousands of choices. California has become one of the world's leading wine producers; Washington, Oregon, and New York State are producing more excellent wines in all price ranges; and now very fine wineries have developed in almost every region of the United States. But sometimes it can be very difficult to find some of these wines. Indeed, thanks in large part to the legacy of Prohibition, shopping for wine in the United States can be complicated and sometimes frustrating. I'll explain why a little bit later in the chapter.

I hope this section will be helpful for those who are interested in developing their own taste, building their own wine collection, or looking for a good bottle of wine for tonight's dinner. Let's begin by learning how the wine industry works, examining how it came to work this way, and exploring the primary ways consumers can purchase wine.

Most Americans buy wine either in retail wine and liquor stores or in restaurants. Buying wine in a retail store sounds simple enough: You walk in looking for wine. You're either shopping for a specific wine or looking for a new wine to try out with your dinner. The point is, you want to buy wine and you're looking forward to enjoying it.

That simple shopping trip is often very frustrating, however. Buyers are often unable to find the year, label, or type of wine they're looking for. Instead they're confronted with an almost overwhelming choice of wines, many of which they know nothing about.

Why doesn't the wine shop have the exact bottle you want? Because wine retailing is different from most other retailing in the United States.

Wine Retailing

Small producers from the fifty states, not to mention all over the world, produce wines in limited quantities. Because their supply is limited, your ability to find exactly what you're looking for is chancy. The store you're shopping in might be sold out of the wine you want or might never have stocked the wine. In fact, it might never even have been offered the opportunity to purchase the wine in the first place.

Second, unlike food, clothing, or electronics, no national retail or distribution network exists for wines—and that's because of some uniquely American history.

Prohibition 1920–33

As discussed earlier, Prohibition taught the federal government that prohibiting the sale and consumption of alcoholic beverages created far more problems than it solved: U.S. citizens wanted their alcohol and they were going to have it. Crime rates rose and tax revenues fell. Still, upon repeal of Prohibition, the federal government took a very cautious approach to regulating the sale and distribution of all alcoholic beverages. Instead of setting up laws on a federal level, Congress decided to let individual states legislate intrastate and interstate distribution.

The result of this decision is that each of the fifty states has different rules and regulations, creating an enormous challenge for wine producers—foreign and domestic—in bringing their wines to market. In New York State, for example, an individual can buy a retail liquor license to operate a retail liquor store. That shop will be allowed to sell only wine and spirits, not beer. Supermarkets in New York are allowed to sell beer, but not wine or spirits. Across the river in New Jersey, there are many places you can buy food and wine in the same store. In Pennsylvania, wine and liquor stores are run by the state, not by individuals, and state authority sets pricing and selection policies. Some states make matters even worse by allowing individual counties and even municipalities within the state to set up their own rules. As you can imagine, this makes the distribution of wines and spirits in the United States an extremely complex business.

Wine Distribution

Given the complexity of a fifty-state system, most states use the three-tier system of distribution. The system was designed to allow for areas of specialization along the cumbersome path of getting wine to consumers.

THE THREE TIERS ARE:

Tier I—Importers and wineries
Tier II—Wholesalers and/or distributors
Tier III—Retailers and restaurants

Tier I—Importers and Wineries: The first tier comprises importers and wineries. A winery is self-explanatory: These are the winemakers who actually make the wines you buy in a wine shop or enjoy in a restaurant. The largest portion of all wine produced in the United States is sold by wineries directly to second-tier wholesalers.

Importers are buyers. They select wines from producers all over the world, sometimes entering into exclusive arrangements with them, negotiating prices, and shipping wines into the United States.

There are also importers that represent some American wineries nationally.

Tier II—Wholesalers and/or Distributors: The second tier of wine distribution belongs to wholesalers and/or distributors. One of their functions is dealing with all the rules and regulations of the state in which they reside. Some wholesalers/distributors operate in multiple states and have an intricate knowledge of the rules and regulations in many states. Wholesalers also play a key role in determining price. Negotiating with importers and wineries (remember, most wine is first brought to market through either importers or wineries), wholesalers negotiate how much they'll pay for each bottle they handle. They then sell directly to retail stores and restaurants.

Mergers and acquisitions have turned what used to be small mom-and-pop wholesale businesses into major corporate delivery systems of wines to retailers and restaurants. For example, Southern Wines and Spirits, which began as a wholesaler in Florida, was, in 2006, operating in twelve states. The Charmer-Sunbelt Group, which began in New York, has wholesale operations in sixteen states.

It's not important for individual wine buyers to

know the names of wholesalers. They're key players for the first and third tiers: wineries and importers, and retailers and restaurants. To the consumer, they're all but invisible.

Tier III—Retailers and Restaurants: The retailer and the restaurateur are the best-known links in the wine distribution system in the United States, the links most familiar to wine consumers all across the country, and the links most important for you to understand.

Wine consumers have several different options when it comes to buying wine. The most common options are:

- Retail stores
- Restaurants
- Wineries
- Wine clubs
- Wine auctions
- The Internet

Because of the different laws of each of the fifty states, it's impossible to be specific about how you can buy wine in your particular state, county, or municipality. From this point on, I'll describe the ways most generally available to wine buyers throughout the country, and I'll give general advice about buying wine, which should be useful regardless of where you do your buying. But first, let's take a look at pricing.

Wine Prices

A winery will determine its prices by taking into account its overhead, production and marketing costs, and the availability of and demand for the wine, then look to make some profit. Next, the winery

sells its wine to the wholesaler. The wholesaler has to cover the cost he's paid the winery as well as warehousing, shipping, other expenses, and, of course, include his profit. He then sells to the retailer and restaurateur. The retailer or restaurateur buying the wine determines the final price that you, the consumer, will pay.

Retail pricing in wine is similar to other retail businesses. There are no fixed rules and no standard markups. But general policies do exist. Full markup equals 50 percent of what the retailer pays for the wine. In a competitive marketplace, some retailers sell wines at significantly lower markups. The average markup probably runs between 25 percent and 35 percent.

Retailers can use pricing as a marketing tool: Sometimes retailers sell popular wines at a lower markup—or even at cost, where permissible—as a lure to bring customers into the store, hoping that they'll buy other items at a higher markup as well. Some retailers discount prices as a matter of policy, appealing directly to the cost-conscious wine consumer. And since most wine is meant to be consumed within one year, retailers often put old or slow-selling stock on sale to clean out their inventory and make room for new wines.

The size and selection of the store, its location, and the knowledge of the owners and staff and the service they provide also determine pricing. If you are a serious wine buyer, find a good retailer in your area and develop a relationship with the staff. As a regular customer, you will get better pricing, good advice, and the most current information on wines you're likely to enjoy.

Remember, too, that wine is a precious commodity; good wines are not mass produced. Vineyard owners are essentially farmers, and their ability to produce top-quality wines depends on rain, temperature, healthy crops, and good fortune.

Wine Retail Store Options

Given that state laws vary, there are generally four types of outlets that sell wine at retail. They are:

1 Supermarkets and grocery stores
2 National retail chains
3 Other retail outlets
4 Wine and liquor stores

Supermarkets and Grocery Stores: A tremendous amount of wine is sold in supermarkets. Some wine publications even track total monthly wine sales in supermarkets broken down by varietals and style, to give an indication of overall national sales. The biggest advantage of buying wine in supermarkets is convenience: You can buy your wine at the same time and in the same place you're buying your groceries. Supermarkets often offer decent wines at reasonable prices. However, with some notable exceptions, supermarkets tend to offer a limited selection, often stocking only the most mass-produced and marketed varieties. These can be perfectly satisfying wines, but you'll have to do your own homework by buying and trying. Because wine is not their primary business, these stores seldom have knowledgeable staff and are unlikely to offer any special ordering service. But if your wine-buying retail choices are limited or you just prefer the convenience, try to shop in a supermarket where the selection shows some quality. Those are likely to be supermarkets with knowledgeable wine managers. Get to know the wine manager. Listen to his recommendations and if you find them satisfying, use him as a resource in trying new wines.

National Retail Chains: Where state laws permit, national retail chains have begun selling wine. Since their core business is focused on discount, it's possible to find some good wines at very good prices. Still, they are most likely to offer limited selections featuring the best-selling wines. Costco is the number one retailer of wine in the United States with more than $300 million in sales.

Other Retail Outlets: Drug stores, gas stations, and convenience stores are useful when there are no other alternatives. Prices can be attractive, but selections are likely to be very limited. If you're serious about wine, these are not retailers you'll be doing a lot of business with. Still, for wines under $20, they will probably have something worth buying.

Wine and Liquor Stores: Fortunately for the majority of wine consumers, there are retailers who specialize in wine. The staff members read the wine trade journals and are often familiar with vintages, producers, importers, vineyards, varietals, and blends from all over the world. They might sell wine exclusively, or they might be full-service wine, liquor, and beer stores. The heart and soul of the wine industry, wine stores are often owned and staffed by dedicated wine professionals. They take a keen interest in all the wines they carry, care about the tastes and demands of their customers, and will go out of their way to help you find a bottle of that special wine you had at a restaurant the night before. These are the shops you want to haunt. Get to know the staff, their tastes, and let them get to know you. The more they learn about your wine preferences, the more likely they are to recommend wines that will suit your tastes and to introduce you to wines you might not have otherwise tried.

An established relationship with a good wine retailer can also provide access to hard-to-find wines. Take California Cabernet Sauvignon as an example. There are more than 1,600 wineries in California and hundreds of them produce Cabernet Sauvignon. Some of the best and most sought after Cabernets are allocated by the producers to a few select retailers. Those retailers are given an allotment of wine—even they don't have an unlimited supply—which they offer only to their preferred customers. If you don't have a strong relationship with that retailer, you won't be able to buy the wine.

Choose a wine retailer with the same care and consideration you would use in choosing a great restaurant, an understanding therapist, a skilled doctor, an experienced lawyer, or a creative hairdresser.

Sampling Before Buying

This sounds like a great concept and follows my rule never to buy a case of wine until I've tried a bottle, but it can be problematic. While many grocers provide

samples, the types of samples offered are limited, and what is offered is often provided by the producer as a form of marketing.

Sampling exists in many wine shops in the form of wine tastings. Tastings are often supported by importers or wineries; they want you to try their wine, hoping you'll like it enough to buy a bottle—or more.

Quality wine retailers often host their own wine tastings, sometimes providing the wine themselves. There are also wine shops throughout the country that offer wine classes. Those retailers are committed to introducing their regular customers to new types and varieties of wine. They understand that everything in wine is about taste: If you like it, you'll buy it.

Of course, those pesky state regulations also play an important role in whether a store can offer wine samples. Remember, different states have different rules. Nineteen states prohibit any wine sampling in retail outlets, while fifteen other states impose a variety of restrictions.

Making Sense of Wine Ratings

Ratings are a fact of life in America, and it was inevitable that rating systems would come to the wine industry. If you understand how wine-rating systems work, you can use them to your advantage. Ratings began in the wine trade as a twenty-point scoring system to establish uniform standards at professional wine tastings. The twenty-point system assigns a numerical value to each of four qualities that professional wine tasters judge when they taste wine. As you look at how the points are allotted, you'll see what qualities professionals look for in a wine and how important each quality is in the over-all rating. In the twenty-point system, each quality and its maximum value is:

Color and appearance	3
Smell (aroma and bouquet)	5
Taste (flavor)	9
Length and quality	3
	20 points

Consumer wine ratings began with a hundred-point system developed by the wine writer Robert M. Parker Jr. In the hundred-point system, every wine begins with fifty points. As the quality of the wine increases, so does the number of points it re-ceives—all the way up to an orgasmic one hundred points! Nearly all wine publications and most wine critics have now adopted the hundred-point system. It's the system you're most likely to encounter in wine shops, catalogs, books, and magazines.

Opinions are divided on whether this is the best way to judge wine. Personally, I have no use for rating wine by numbers and believe you should judge wine by whether or not you like it. For con-sumers, a high rating gives credibility to a wine's quality. But be cautious in relying solely on ratings: If you consider eighty points a low rating, you might ignore well-made, reasonably priced wines with characteristics you would find appealing without breaking the bank.

You will encounter ratings as you shop for wine, whether in retail stores, on the Internet, in catalogs, or through wine clubs, so learn to use ratings to your best advantage. Study the critics with rating systems, choose the ones whose tastes most match your own, and buy accordingly. But keep in mind that critics are individuals too. As with movie critics, book reviewers, and restaurant reviewers, no one critic's opinion will ever exactly match your own.

Restaurants

The strong growth in wine consumption in the United States has affected the restaurant business dramatically. Wine lists are no longer the province of an elite group of high-ticket, white-tablecloth culinary temples. There are ever-increasing ranks of customers who actively seek to enjoy wine of all price levels in restaurants.

As a result, wine service has improved tremendously in American restaurants over the last thirty years. Diners are far more likely today to find intelligently crafted wine lists that complement the chef's food, along with waiters and waitresses who are better prepared to recommend wine-and-food pairings than ever before in the United States. Diners should expect at least this much from any restaurant they patronize. I advise everyone to apply the same care in choosing a restaurant—its food, service, and wine list—as I do in finding a good retail wine store.

One of the biggest challenges in dining out with a large group is choosing wine that matches a wide variety of main courses: meat, fish, and vegetarian selections.

I recommend ordering "safe" wines. My favorite choice for white wine is Chardonnay, either without oak or slightly oak aged, or an unoaked Sauvignon

- Not enough wine lists for the number of tables
- Incorrect information, i.e., wrong vintage and producer
- High markups
- Untrained staff
- Lack of corkscrews
- Out-of-stock wines
- Improper glassware
- Overchilled whites and warm reds

Blanc. As for the reds, my number one choice is definitely a Pinot Noir, especially from California or Oregon. These selections work well with meat, fish, and vegetarian choices.

Wine by the glass is the best thing that has happened to wine appreciation for both consumers and restaurateurs. Smith & Wollensky's restaurants, for instance, sold more than one million individually ordered glasses of wine in 2006!

As a consumer, I only experiment with wine in a restaurant that has a good selection of wines by the glass or half bottle. This also eliminates the challenge of choosing a bottle of wine when one dinner

guest orders fish and another orders meat. You won't get stuck trying to choose one bottle that will accommodate everyone's different menu choices.

Buying Direct from Wineries

Buying wine at wineries can be fun and exciting. A tour of your local winery provides great scenery, good food, and a real education in how wine is made. You'll gain a better understanding of why each vineyard in a similar geographic area produces a unique product. You'll discover labels you may not know and find varietals that are often impossible to buy anywhere but at the source. You'll meet the growers and begin to understand the kind of passion, commitment, dedication, pride, and love they have for their grapes, their fields, their vocation, and their wine. Your knowledge of wine and appreciation of its complexities will expand exponentially. I encourage all wine enthusiasts to visit as many vineyards in as many regions and countries as possible. Visiting the source is a soulful experience. Plus, you get to actually taste the wine before you buy it!

But be mindful of how much you buy; the law in your state might limit you to what you can carry home. Shipping wine is subject to the same set of archaic rules and regulations that apply to the sale and transportation of all alcoholic beverages. Check your state, county, or local laws to find out whether you're legally allowed to have wine shipped to your home.

If you live in Southern California, you're in luck if you'd like to tour the North Coast wineries of Napa and Sonoma, taste some excellent wines, and decide to have them shipped to your home—intrastate shipping is perfectly legal. Many other states allow you to ship wine from California as well. But there are some states where direct shipment from out of state is prohibited.

Many of these laws will be changing, thanks to a recent Supreme Court ruling. But it will take time for these changes to take effect, so, for the time being, check with the winery or liquor control board before you make plans to ship any wine across state lines.

2005 Supreme Court Decision
(*Granholm v. Heald*)

In May 2005 the Supreme Court, in a 5–4 ruling, struck down laws in New York and Michigan as discriminatory because they allow in-state wineries, but not out-of-state wineries, to ship directly to consumers. The cases were brought to the Supreme Court on appeal, with the plaintiffs claiming that the state laws discriminated against out-of-state wineries and therefore violated the U.S. Constitution's commerce clause, which prohibits states from intruding in interstate commerce. The states argued that they did in fact have powers to regulate alcoholic beverages, citing the Twenty-first Amendment to the U.S. Constitution, which, when enacted in 1933, repealed Prohibition.

The clear effect of the recent Supreme Court ruling is that as many as twenty-four states that currently bar out-of-state shipments will have to revise their laws so wineries are treated equally. This decision makes specific laws in six other states—Connecticut, Florida, Indiana, Massachusetts, Ohio, and Vermont—invalid, as are the reciprocity laws thirteen states had enacted to allow for direct shipping between them. These states include California, Colorado, Hawaii, Idaho, Illinois, Iowa, Minnesota, Missouri, New Mexico, Oregon, Washington, West

Virginia, and Wisconsin. Again, the Court's ruling does not in itself effect any changes, but it requires the state legislatures to revisit their laws. If you have a problem buying wine in your state, contact your state legislator or representative. The distribution from wineries throughout the United States will still depend on what each state legislature does. The impact of the ruling for now is that states must "level the playing field" and treat in-state and out-of-state wineries similarly.

In the case of New York State, a law was soon enacted to allow residents to buy directly from out-of-state wineries, whereas before they could only buy from New York producers.

Wine Clubs

Wine clubs exist to provide wine consumers with an easy way to purchase wine without leaving home. Wine clubs offer many types of service: Some automatically ship new wines to you each month; some offer special "club discounts"; some offer proprietary brands; some offer rare wines; and some clubs offer wine novices an introduction to the entire world of wine by automatically selecting and shipping a selection of different wines—red, white, foreign, and domestic—each month. I did a quick Internet search for "wine clubs" and found more than three hundred listings.

My experience with wine clubs has been disappointing; I didn't find that they offered a better selection than a good wine retailer, and the rules and conditions of membership often aren't worth the trouble. But if you prefer the convenience of armchair shopping, look for a club that offers exactly what you're looking for, whether it's low price, automatic selection, or a wine education by mail.

The same interstate shipping rules apply to clubs

that apply to all wine shipping. As you investigate club buying, first check to make sure the club can legally ship wine to you.

If you've thought about joining a wine club but your state doesn't allow delivery of out-of-state wines, there are other options. Check with your local wine retailer. Many have existing clubs and Web sites; those that don't will often set up a club just for you. Let your retailer know what you want: Describe your favorite wine color, regions, and price range, and decide how many bottles you want each month. Some retailers offer delivery to your door of wine especially selected for you and your taste.

Investing in Wine

It wasn't long ago that outstanding California wines could find few buyers beyond serious wine collectors, who are always in pursuit of new wines, looking for wines that they believe are underappreciated and undervalued. These same collectors, after tasting the extraordinary Cabernet vintages of the early 1990s, realized the potential for these wines in the fine-wine market, and they bought all they could get. They brought the world's attention and focus to California wines, introducing the larger market of individual consumers to California's outstanding product, while simultaneously increasing the value of their own California wine holdings. Now, because of the keen noses of those early collectors, the great vintages from the best producers of California Cabernet Sauvignon sell out very quickly. Nearly the entire productions are bought by "new" wine collectors who are buying wines either to enjoy at a later date or to sell at a profit at auction in five years.

Market conditions today are different from what they were even five years ago: In the last ten years there have been only five great investment-grade vintages in California wine. Investment-grade wines aren't produced with predictable regularity. As with

any speculative venture, investing in wine is risky: You need to be sure you're willing to take a loss if you decide to buy wine solely as an investment. Plus, you'll need to make sure you have the proper facilities in which to store your investment. And, of course, in many states it may still be illegal, at least until the repercussions of the 2005 Supreme Court ruling have settled, for individuals to sell wine without a license. You'll need to check your local laws before considering wine investments.

By all means, buy wine by the case and buy futures if you can afford them. Even if you don't make any money, you'll still have the wine, and while it may not have brought you great wealth, it will be there for you to open, pour, and enjoy.

CHAPTER 4

American Wine State by State

ALABAMA

Most of Alabama's six wineries are clustered in the foothills in the northeast of the state. Some French hybrids are grown, but the majority of Alabama wines are blended Muscadines, native to the region and favored by the Southern palate to drier, less fruity wines. Fruit wines are also made.

Hurricane Katrina brought significant damage to coastal Alabama and destroyed the grape crop. Growers are sourcing out-of-state grapes to make up for the loss of local supply.

Perdido, Alabama's first winery, takes advantage of tourism on the Gulf Coast, sometimes known irreverently as the "redneck Riviera." Perdido pokes fun at this stereotype with its "cou rouge" rosé, featuring a bottle with a miniature red bandanna tied around the bottleneck.

—R.L.

STATE WEB SITE: www.alabamawines.org

NUMBER OF WINERIES: 6

U.S. RANK FOR NUMBER OF BONDED WINERIES: #40

(continued)

Information on the individual states was compiled by contributing editors Becky Sue Epstein (B.S.E.), Richard Leahy (R.L.), Inez Ribustello (I.R.), Steve Topping (S.T.), and Kevin Zraly (K.Z.).

FIRST WINERY: Perdido Vineyards, 1979

LARGEST WINERY: Perdido Vineyards

WELL-KNOWN WINERIES: Bryant Vineyard, Perdido Vineyards, White Oak Vineyards

TOP GRAPES: Muscadines (Noble, Carlos, Scuppernong, Magnolia), Chambourcin, Chardonel, Villard, Cynthiana/Norton

AMERICAN VITICULTURAL AREAS: none

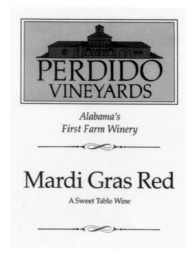

ALASKA

Alaska is too far north for wine-grape viticulture, but its wineries do a thriving trade in native fruit and honey-based wines, as well as with blended wines using juice from outside the state. Bear Creek Winery, a small winery with an eight-thousand-bottle production, is open year-round and reports "very busy" visitation from Memorial Day to Labor Day, with ten thousand estimated visitors per year. They "pick, buy, and trade" for local berries, apples, and rhubarb, sourcing grape concentrate for fermenting from wherever they can find it.

—R.L.

STATE WEB SITE: www.americanwineries.org

NUMBER OF WINERIES: 6

U.S. RANK FOR NUMBER OF BONDED WINERIES: #42

FIRST WINERY: Denali Winery, 1997

LARGEST WINERY: Denali Winery

WELL-KNOWN WINERIES: Alaskan Wilderness Wines, Kodiak Island Winery, Bear Creek Winery

TOP GRAPES: Only grape juice sourced from outside the state and local fruits and honey products are used for wine.

AMERICAN VITICULTURAL AREAS: none

ALC 11% BY VOLUME

Rhubarb
Produced & Bottled by
Steven & Lisa Thomsen in Kodiak, Alaska

ARIZONA

Dr. Gordon Dutt, a soil scientist at the University of Arizona, became so convinced that grapes would grow well in Sonoita, southeast of Tucson, that he took his own advice and started Sonoita Vineyards. His success attracted several other winemakers to Sonoita, which is Arizona's sole AVA.

—S.T.

State Web site: www.arizonawine.org

Number of wineries: 17

U.S. rank for number of bonded wineries: #26

First winery: Sonoita Vineyards, 1983

Largest winery: Kokopelli Winery

Well-known wineries: Callaghan Vineyards, Dos Cabezas Wineworks, Kokopelli Winery, Sonoita Vineyards

Top grapes: Cabernet Sauvignon, Pinot Noir, Viognier, Sauvignon Blanc

American viticultural area: 1—Sonoita

ARKANSAS

Said to be the oldest and largest wine-producing state in the South, Arkansas is home to five federally bonded wineries. The most recent addition is The Winery in Hot Springs, having just opened in 2006. Cowie Wine Cellars is the only winery located outside of Altus, and it is home to the Arkansas Historic Wine Museum. Beginning in 1899, Arkansas has held the "Grape Festival" that continues to attract locals and tourists today.

—I.R.

STATE WEB SITE: www.americanwineries.org

NUMBER OF WINERIES: 5

U.S. RANK FOR NUMBER OF BONDED WINERIES: #43

FIRST WINERIES: Post Familie Vineyards, Wiederkehr Wine Cellars, both in 1880

LARGEST WINERIES: Wiederkehr Wine Cellars

WELL-KNOWN WINERIES: Chateau Aux Arc, Cowie Wine Cellars, Mount Bethel Winery, Post Familie Vineyard, Wiederkehr Wine Cellars

TOP GRAPES: Chardonnay, Zinfandel, Cabernet Sauvignon, Cynthiana/Norton, Vidal, Vignoles, Muscadine, Catawba, Carlos, Noble, Munson, Niagara

AMERICAN VITICULTURAL AREAS: 3—Altus, Arkansas Mountain, Ozark Mountain

PREMIUM WINEMAKERS

Post Familie

VINEYARDS

WHITE
MUSCADINE

SEMI SWEET
ALCOHOL 12
BY VOLUME

Wiederkehr®

Altus

CABERNET SAUVIGNON

*Rare, dry red table wine with delightful color,
bouquet and robust flavor of the famous Cabernet
Sauvignon grape vine. Enjoy at room temperature
with almost any foods. Best with red meats or cheese.*

*Made and Bottled by Wiederkehr Wine Cellars,
Inc. Altus, Arkansas.* B.W.C. No.8 *Alcohol 12% by Volume.*

M-124   ATP

CALIFORNIA

If California were a country, it would be the fourth largest wine producer in the world! In the early seventies when I first started studying about wines, there were only a handful of wineries that produced quality wine. Today California has more than 1,600 wineries producing some of the finest wines in the world. And the best is yet to come!

See Chapter 5 for more detailed information about California wines and winemaking.

—K.Z.

State Web site: www.wineinstitute.org

Number of wineries: 1,658

U.S. rank for number of wineries: #1

First winery: Buena Vista Winery, 1857

Largest winery: Gallo

Well-known wineries: See Chapter 5

Acres of vines: 800,000 +

U.S. rank for acres of vines: #1

Top grapes:
Cabernet Sauvignon
Chardonnay
Merlot
Syrah
Sauvignon Blanc
Pinot Noir

(continued)

CLOS PEGASE

MITSUKO'S VINEYARD
SAUVIGNON BLANC
CARNEROS • NAPA VALLEY
ESTATE BOTTLED

ALC. 13.9% BY VOL.

ROBERT MONDAVI

NAPA VALLEY

FUMÉ BLANC

ALCOHOL 12.5% BY VOLUME

PINOT NOIR

Sea Smoke

BOTELLA

APPELLATION SANTA RITA HILLS

Santa Barbara County California

750ML 14.1% ALC/VOL

NEWTON

CHARDONNAY

NAPA COUNTY 60% / SONOMA COUNTY 40%

PRODUCED AND BOTTLED BY NEWTON VINEYARD ST HELENA CALIFORNIA ALC 14.5%/VOL. PRODUCT OF USA ©

Alexander Valley
Alta Mesa
Anderson Valley
Arroyo Grande Valley
Arroyo Seco
Atlas Peak
Ben Lomond
  Mountain
Benmore Valley
Bennett Valley
Borden Ranch
California
  Shenandoah Valley
Capay Valley
Carmel Valley
Central Coast
Chalk Hill
Chalone
Chiles Valley
Cienega Valley
Clarksburg
Clear Lake
Clement Hills
Cole Ranch
Consumnes River
Covelo
Cucamonga Valley
Diablo Grande
Diamond Mountain
Dos Rios
Dry Creek Valley
Dunnigan Hills
Edna Valley
El Dorado
Fair Play
Fiddletown
Guenoc Valley
Hames Valley
High Valley
Howell Mountain
Jahant

(continued)

PETER MICHAEL
· WINERY ·

'L' APRÈS-MIDI'

SONOMA COUNTY SAUVIGNON BLANC ◆ ALCOHOL 14.2% BY VOLUME
ESTATE BOTTLED BY PETER MICHAEL
CALISTOGA, CA USA

RAVENS

W O O D

TELDESCHI
ZINFANDEL
DRY CREEK VALLEY

ALCOHOL 14.9% BY VOL.

RIDGE 2002
CALIFORNIA
MONTE BELLO®

MONTE BELLO VINEYARD: 74% CABERNET SAUVIGNON,
18% MERLOT, 8% PETIT VERDOT
SANTA CRUZ MOUNTAINS   ALCOHOL 13.3% BY VOLUME
GROWN, PRODUCED & BOTTLED BY RIDGE VINEYARDS
17100 MONTE BELLO ROAD, BOX 1810, CUPERTINO, CA 95015

Knights Valley
Lime Kiln Valley
Livermore Valley
Lodi
Los Carneros
Madera
Malibu-Newton
  Canyon
McDowell Valley
Mendocino
Mendocino Ridge
Merritt Island
Mokelumne River
Monterey
Mount Harlan
Mount Veeder
Napa Valley
North Coast
North Yuba
Northern Sonoma
Oak Knoll District
Oakville
Pacheco Pass
Paicines
Paso Robles
Potter Valley
Ramona Valley
Red Hills Lake
  County
Redwood Valley
River Junction
Rockpile
Russian River Valley
Rutherford
Saddle Rock-Malibu
Salado Creek
San Antonio
San Benito
San Bernabe

(continued)

NAPA VALLEY
CABERNET SAUVIGNON
PRODUCED AND BOTTLED BY
Mayacamas Vineyards
NAPA, CALIFORNIA, U.S.A. ALCOHOL 12½% BY VOLUME

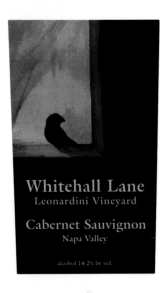

Whitehall Lane
Leonardini Vineyard

Cabernet Sauvignon
Napa Valley

alcohol 14.2% by vol.

CAIN FIVE
NAPA VALLEY

CABERNET SAUVIGNON 52%
PETIT VERDOT 20%
CABERNET FRANC 14%
MERLOT 9%
MALBEC 5%

San Francisco Bay
San Lucas
San Pasqual Valley
San Ysidro District
Santa Clara Valley
Santa Cruz
  Mountains
Santa Lucia
  Highlands
Santa Maria Valley
Santa Rita Hills
Santa Ynez Valley
Seiad Valley
Sierra Foothills
Sloughhouse
Solano County
  Green Valley
Sonoma Coast
Sonoma County
  Green Valley
Sonoma Mountain
Sonoma Valley
South Coast
Spring Mountain
  District
St. Helena
Stags Leap District
Suisun Valley
Temecula Valley
Trinity Lakes
Wild Horse Valley
Willow Creek
York Mountain
Yorkville Highlands
Yountville

MERRYVALE

STARMONT
CHARDONNAY

NAPA VALLEY

ALC. 13.5 % BY VOL.

IRON HORSE
VINEYARDS

ESTATE BOTTLED
Chardonnay

SONOMA COUNTY-GREEN VALLEY

ALC. 14.4% BY VOL.

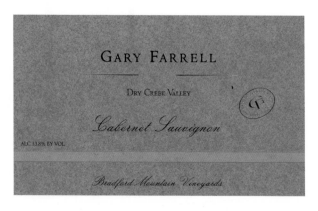

GARY FARRELL

DRY CREEK VALLEY

Cabernet Sauvignon

ALC. 13.8% BY VOL.

Bradford Mountain Vineyards

GRGICH HILLS

Napa Valley
CABERNET SAUVIGNON

PRODUCED AND BOTTLED BY
GRGICH HILLS CELLAR, RUTHERFORD, CA

Cakebread
Cellars

CABERNET SAUVIGNON
Benchland Select
NAPA VALLEY

Jack Cakebread

ALC. 14.1% VOL.

La Jota Vineyard Co
ESTATE

NAPA VALLEY - HOWELL MOUNTAIN
Cabernet Sauvignon
ANNIVERSARY

ANNIVERSARY RELEASE

CHALK HILL
2001 ESTATE BOTTLED
CABERNET SAUVIGNON
CHALK HILL, SONOMA COUNTY

Frederick and Peggy Furth, Proprietors

COLORADO

Colorado had a thriving wine industry interrupted by Prohibition. Grapes were not replanted commercially until the late 1970s, but since then Colorado winemakers have been making up for lost time, with the number of wineries in the state quintupling in the last ten years.

Many of the vineyards and wineries are clustered around Palisade, located along the Colorado River's Grand Valley (AVA) on the western slope of the Continental Divide, accounting for some 80 percent of Colorado's grapes. Colorado's other AVA, West Elks, along the North Fork of the Gunnison River, is about a thousand feet higher in elevation.

High altitude and a semi-arid climate distinguish Colorado's growing conditions. The season is marked by hot, sunny days and cooler nights, and can be shortened by freezes at beginning or end. The dry climate causes the growers to depend on irrigation, so, as they like to say in the region, they have moisture when they need it, and not when they don't.

The Grand Valley resembles France's Rhône Valley, and so winemakers have been increasing their production of Syrah. Look for them to begin to focus also on Viognier, the Rhône's white grape. Riesling has seen the most new plantings, especially in the West Elks AVA. Carlson Vineyards' 2003 Riesling won the World Riesling Cup at the 28th International Eastern Wine Competition, one of the oldest and most prestigious competitions in the United States, becoming the first Colorado winery to earn any Riesling award, let alone the top prize. Perhaps it should come as no surprise that the following year more Riesling was planted in Colorado than any other variety.

—S.T

State Web site: www.coloradowine.com

Number of wineries: 57

U.S. rank for number of bonded wineries: #12

First winery: Ivancie Winery, 1968

Largest winery: Colorado Cellars

Well-known wineries: Bookcliff Vineyards, Boulder Creek Winery, Canyon Wind Cellars, Carlson Vineyards, Cottonwood Cellars, Alfred Eames Cellars, Garfield Estates, Grande River Vineyards, Mountain Spirit, Plum Creek Cellars, Spero, Sutcliffe Vineyards, and Two Rivers Winery

Top grapes: Merlot, Chardonnay, Syrah, Riesling, Cabernet Sauvignon

American viticultural areas: 2—Grand Valley, West Elks

Best Bets: 2004, 2005* for all, but especially whites

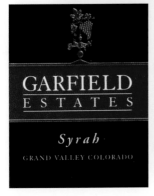

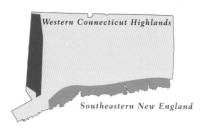

Western Connecticut Highlands

Southeastern New England

CONNECTICUT

This state concentrates on European-style wines and grapes more than other states in the Northeast. The owner of Connecticut's first vineyard, Haight, maintains he was determined to grow traditional wine grapes (*Vitis vinifera*) more than thirty years ago when he was told it couldn't be done in this state. After some years—and some expensive siting mistakes—Haight's Riesling and Chardonnay wines are still winning medals. Over the years, twenty other adventurous people have followed in his footsteps, and ten more wineries and vineyards are in the start-up phase.

—B.S.E.

STATE WEB SITE: www.ctwine.com

NUMBER OF WINERIES: 20

U.S. RANK FOR NUMBER OF BONDED WINERIES: #24

FIRST WINERY: Haight Vineyard, 1978

LARGEST WINERY: Sharpe Hill

WELL-KNOWN WINERIES: Chamard, Di Grazia, Hopkins, Priam, Sharpe Hill, Stonington

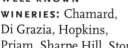

HAIGHT
BLANC DE BLANCS
METHODE CHAMPENOISE
SPARKLING WINE
produced & bottled by Haight Vineyard
LITCHFIELD, CONNECTICUT
ALCOHOL 12.5% BY VOLUME

TOP GRAPES:
Chardonnay, Cabernet Franc, Riesling, Seyval Blanc, St. Croix, Vidal

AMERICAN VITICULTURAL AREAS:
2—Southeastern New England, Western Connecticut Highlands

WINE TRAILS:

Southeastern New England Growing Appellation,
Eastern Trail: The Connecticut Shore, Western
Trail: The Connecticut Highlands

Delaware

Delaware's wineries take advantage of the substantial tourist traffic to the local beaches. Well-established Nassau Valley Vineyards hosts a range of attractions, including weddings, private parties, corporate events, and summer concerts.

The sandy soil suits Cabernet Sauvignon, especially in dry years, and Chardonnay also performs well. In wet years, French hybrids like Seyval Blanc and Chambourcin are more reliable. Seyval Blanc seems to produce the most terroir-driven wine, with grapefruit-like flavors and acidity. Award-winning fruit wines such as blueberry are also produced.

—R.L.

State Web site: www.americanwineries.org

Number of wineries: 2

U.S. rank for number of bonded wineries: #50

First winery: Nassau Valley Vineyards, 1993

Largest winery: Nassau Valley Vineyards

Well-known winery: Nassau Valley Vineyards

Top grapes: Chardonnay, Cabernet Sauvignon, Seyval Blanc, Chambourcin

American viticultural areas: none

FLORIDA

From the Panhandle down to Homestead at the southern tip, there are wineries spanning the state. Very few *Vitis vinifera* grapes are grown in Florida, though scientists are researching the possibility of future *vinifera* vineyards. Many of the wines are made from fruits such as oranges, lychees, and mangoes, but there are also plenty of wines made from Muscadine. Carlos is the main white varietal, and Noble is the primary red varietal.

—I.R.

STATE WEB SITE: www.fgga.org

NUMBER OF WINERIES: 30

U.S. RANK FOR NUMBER OF BONDED WINERIES: #16

FIRST WINERY:
Lakeridge Winery & Vineyards, 1989

LARGEST WINERY:
Lakeridge Winery & Vineyards

WELL-KNOWN WINERIES:
Chautauqua Winery, Henscratch Winery, Lakeridge Winery & Vineyards, San Sebastian, St. Augustine

TOP GRAPES:
Muscadine, Blanc du Bois, Stover, Conquistador

AMERICAN VITICULTURAL AREAS: none

GEORGIA

Georgia is the largest producer of Muscadine in the United States. The state has a very diverse setup as far as terrain is concerned. In the mountains of Georgia, many *vinifera* varietals are grown such as Roussanne and Cabernet Sauvignon, and in the warmer, flatter areas, peaches and other fruits flourish. These very unique microclimates allow Georgia to grow a variety of fruits that make wines from dry to sticky sweet.

—I.R.

STATE WEB SITES: www.georgiawinecouncil.org, www.georgiawinecountry.com

NUMBER OF WINERIES: 18

U.S. RANK FOR NUMBER OF BONDED WINERIES: #25

First winery: Georgia Winery, 1983

Largest winery: Château Élan

Well-known wineries: Château Élan Winery,
Frogtown Cellars Winery, Habersham Vineyards,
Three Sisters Vineyards, Tiger Mountain Vineyards

Top grapes:
Cabernet Franc,
Merlot, Cabernet Sauvignon,
Chardonnay,
Muscadine

American viticultural areas:
none

HAWAII

Hawaii doubled its wineries from two to four in the last year. The two established wineries are Tedeschi on Maui and Volcano Winery on the Big Island, located three miles from Volcano National Park, between two active volcanoes. Located between nineteen and twenty degrees latitude (Volcano Winery touts itself as "America's southernmost winery"), limited viticulture is still possible at higher elevations (greater than 1,500 feet) in the Hawaiian Islands where cool ocean breezes and suitable grape varieties can make it successful.

Fruit wines are popular local products in most of the United States, and Hawaii is no exception; the state's wineries produce no more than 50 percent table wine, with the remainder divided between fruit, fruit/wine blends, and honey-based wines.

—R.L.

STATE WEB SITE: www.americanwineries.org

NUMBER OF WINERIES: 4

U.S. RANK FOR NUMBER OF BONDED WINERIES: #45

FIRST WINERY: Tedeschi Vineyards, 1974

LARGEST WINERY: Tedeschi Vineyards

WELL-KNOWN WINERIES: Tedeschi Vineyards, Volcano Winery

TOP GRAPES: Symphony, Carnelian

AMERICAN VITICULTURAL AREAS: none

MAUI SPLASH
Passion Fruit
Pineapple Wine with natural fruit flavors and caramel coloring

PRODUCED AND BOTTLED BY TEDESCHI VINEYARDS, LTD.
ULUPALAKUA, HAWAII · ALC.11.5% BY VOL · CONT. 750 ML

IDAHO

Idaho's pioneering Ste. Chapelle Winery found its home within view of the Snake River in the southwest part of Idaho, and its success inspired many other winemakers to plant grapes and produce wines in this rich agricultural area known as Sunny Slope.

—S.T.

STATE WEB SITE: www.idahowine.org

NUMBER OF WINERIES: 26

U.S. RANK FOR NUMBER OF BONDED WINERIES: #20

FIRST WINERY: Ste. Chapelle Winery, 1976

LARGEST WINERY: Ste. Chapelle Winery

WELL-KNOWN WINERIES: Camas Prairie, Coeur d'Alene, Parma Ridge, Pend d'Oreille, Sawtooth, Ste. Chapelle Winery, Vickers, Williamson

TOP GRAPES: Riesling, Cabernet Sauvignon, Merlot, Chardonnay

AMERICAN VITICULTURAL AREAS: none

Ste · CHAPELLE

Johannisberg
Riesling
IDAHO

WINEMAKER'S SERIES

Lynfred Winery™

My kind of Wine!

VIN DE CITY RED

American Red Table Wine

ILLINOIS

Illinois was a noted wine-producing region in the mid-nineteenth century. The confluence of the Ohio and Mississippi rivers combined with its rolling hills make Illinois naturally favorable for viticulture, and many of the state's wineries, and its only extant wine trail, are in the southern region.

The town of Nauvoo on the western edge of the state near the Mississippi River was the center of the Illinois wine industry. Baxter's Vineyards/Winery, the oldest winery in the state, dates to this boom period, when six hundred acres of vines were planted near the town. Vaulted wine caves, which can still be seen today, were dug that provided perfect storage conditions. The native Noah grape was first identified here, later planted successfully in New Jersey, then taken to France, where it is still cultivated, and grafted onto European vines because it is resistant to phylloxera.

At the outset of Prohibition, there were more than one million grapevines in the state; after it took effect, Nauvoo's vaulted caves could no longer be openly used for storing wine but were ideal for creating blue cheese. Hence, the new cheese industry replaced wine. Today the Nauvoo Grape Festival, which takes place the weekend before Labor Day, includes a symbolic ceremony based on French tradition, and celebrates the contributions of both wine and cheese to Nauvoo's history and commerce.

The survival of the Illinois wine industry is a

triumph to those passionately committed to the industry, despite the devastating effect on vines of herbicides used widely in the Plains states to kill weeds for annual seed-sown crops.

Illinois has seen a rapid growth in state wineries, acreage of wine grapes planted, quality of wine, and percentage of local wine used in state wines. In 2000, Illinois had only fourteen wineries; today it has fifty-eight, one of the fastest growth rates in the country. The better French hybrids form the backbone of the state industry, and Norton is grown in southern Illinois, the northernmost reaches of its ripening range. Superior Chambourcin is grown, too, with Alto Vineyards leading the way in quality and style. An Illinois specialty is blending Chambourcin with Norton, something other eastern states may learn from. Mary Michelle Winery is pioneering winegrowing made from cross-species hybrids of Norton and *vinifera* grapes.

With its proximity to Chicago and St. Louis, Illinois's wine country benefits from wine tourism. Lynfred Winery, the state's largest winery, near O'Hare Airport, has been particularly successful with an annual Oktoberfest the last weekend of September that draws more than two thousand people.

—R.L.

STATE WEB SITE: www.illinoiswine.com

NUMBER OF WINERIES: 58

U.S. RANK FOR NUMBER OF BONDED WINERIES: #11

FIRST WINERY: Baxter's Vineyards/Winery, 1856

LARGEST WINERY: Lynfred Winery

WELL-KNOWN WINERIES: Alto Vineyards, Galena Cellars, Lynfred Winery, Mary Michelle Winery/Illinois Cellars, Prairie State

TOP GRAPES: Chambourcin, Chardonel, Traminette, Norton, Vidal Blanc, Seyval Blanc, Foch

AMERICAN VITICULTURAL AREAS: none

WINE TRAILS: Shawnee Hills Wine Trail

BEST BETS: 2003, 2004

Ohio River Valley

INDIANA

Indiana is one of many Midwestern states that had vineyards and wineries in the nineteenth century. William Oliver, a law professor at the University of Indiana, used Pennsylvania's farm winery legislation of 1968 as a model for Indiana's farm winery law. After its passage by the legislature in 1972, he opened his own winery, the first in post-Prohibition Indiana. Oliver Winery has since grown into one of the largest noncorporate wineries in the Midwest, with 200,000 cases produced annually. French hybrids and American natives like Catawba are the mainstay of Indiana's wine industry.

Another professional man, physician Charles Thomas, owns Chateau Thomas in Indianapolis. Occasionally he makes some of the best California wines in the country, sourcing fruit from vineyards in Napa and other appellations, and making and finishing the wine at his winery. In 2000 his 1998 Napa Cabernet Franc won Best Red Wine in the International Eastern Wine Competition.

Some wineries have planted Zinfandel, Cabernet Sauvignon, and Cabernet Franc, and red *vinifera* viticulture is promising in the warm Ohio River Valley AVA in the south.

—R.L.

State Web site: www.americanwineries.org

Number of wineries: 30

U.S. rank for number of bonded wineries: #16

First winery: Oliver Winery, 1972

Largest winery: Oliver Winery

Well-known wineries: Chateau Thomas Winery, Easley Winery, French Lick Winery, Huber Orchard & Winery, Oliver Winery

Top grapes: Chambourcin, Traminette, Chardonel, Seyval, Vidal, Vignoles, Foch

American viticultural area: 1—Ohio River Valley

Wine trails: Indiana Uplands Wine Trail

Iowa

Iowa's wine history dates to the nineteenth century with a communal winery model, in this case based on the Amana Colonies, an Amish sect who established ten small wineries around Keokuk. The local specialty was Piestengel, a rhubarb wine. (This heritage is celebrated by the Amana Colonies Wine Trail today.) At the time the hundred-acre White Elk Vineyard had a national reputation for wines based on American varieties like Catawba and Norton.

The vine herbicide 2, 4-D has hampered attempts to reestablish native vineyards, but with education and cooperation from corn and wheat farmers, and state funding for the fledgling industry, viticulture has rebounded in recent years from almost nothing in 2000 to five hundred acres today and thirty-six wineries. Viticulture focuses on cold-hardy hybrids, American varieties, and fruit wines.

—R.L.

State Web sites: www.iowawineandbeer.com

Number of wineries: 36

U.S. rank for number of bonded wineries: #14

First winery: Ehrle Brothers Winery, 1934

Largest winery: Summerset Winery

Well-known wineries: Ackerman Winery, Tabor Home Vineyards & Winery

Top grapes: La Crosse, Edelweiss, La Crescent, St. Croix, Frontenac, Foch, Marquette

American viticultural areas: none

Wine trails: Amana Colonies Wine Trail, Iowa Wine Trail, West Iowa Wine Trail

SUMMERSET WINERY

Caba Moch

Red Table Wine

PRODUCED AND BOTTLED BY SUMMERSET WINERY
1507 FAIRFAX, INDIANOLA, IOWA 50125

KANSAS

On its Web site, Smokey Hill Vineyards and Winery note that most visitors to central Kansas are accustomed to fields of wheat, corn, soybeans, and sunflowers. But grapes grow very well there, too. In fact, Kansas was a major grape-growing state before Prohibition, with some six thousand acres, and these folks are aiming for that amount again. Winemakers have a long way to go, but they've already come far, and people from Kansas are nothing if not determined.

—S.T.

STATE WEB SITE: www.kansasgrapesandwines.com

NUMBER OF WINERIES: 10

U.S. RANK FOR NUMBER OF BONDED WINERIES: #32

FIRST WINERY: Smokey Hill Vineyards and Winery, 1991

LARGEST WINERY: Wyldewood Cellars

WELL-KNOWN WINERIES: Dozier Vineyard & Winery, Holy-Field Vineyard & Winery

TOP GRAPES: Cabernet Franc, Syrah

AMERICAN VITICULTURAL AREAS: none

Ohio River Valley

KENTUCKY

In 1787, Kentucky became one of the first states to establish vineyards, and the state has the oldest vineyard society in America, dating back to 1798. In the 1700s and 1800s, Kentucky was the third largest grape-producing state in America. The Civil War and Prohibition delayed production considerably, though, so farmers chose tobacco as a substitute crop. When tobacco production declined in the 1990s, grape growing reemerged.

—I.R.

STATE WEB SITES: www.kyvineyardsociety.org, www.kywineandvine.com

NUMBER OF WINERIES: 24

U.S. RANK FOR NUMBER OF BONDED WINERIES: #21

FIRST WINERY: Broad Run Vineyards, 1983

LARGEST WINERY: Lover's Leap Vineyard and Winery

WELL-KNOWN WINERIES: Broad Run Vineyards, Equus Run Vineyards, Lover's Leap Vineyard and Winery, Smith Berry Winery, Springhill Winery and Plantation

TOP GRAPES:
Cabernet Sauvignon, Merlot, Riesling, Cabernet Franc, Viognier, Vidal Blanc, Chambourcin, Norton/Cynthiana, Traminette, Chardonel

AMERICAN VITICULTURAL AREA: 1—Ohio River Valley

EQUUS RUN VINEYARDS

Mississippi Delta

LOUISIANA

Between Hurricane Katrina and House Bill 338 outlawing wineries to sell directly to retailers and restaurants, the Louisiana wine industry hasn't been given much of a break. Despite these setbacks, Louisiana's seven wineries seem to forge ahead, continuing to make wines from Muscadine, Blanc du Bois, and Norton grapes.

—I.R.

STATE WEB SITE: www.louisianawines.com

NUMBER OF WINERIES: 7

U.S. RANK FOR NUMBER OF BONDED WINERIES: #35

FIRST WINERY: Casa De Sue Winery, 1992

LARGEST WINERY: Feliciana Cellars

WELL-KNOWN WINERIES: Amato's, Casa De Sue Winery, Feliciana Cellars, Ponchartrain, St. Amant

TOP GRAPES: Muscadine, Niagara, Blanc du Bois, Norton

AMERICAN VITICULTURAL AREA: 1—Mississippi Delta

FELICIANA CELLARS

Galvez

LOUISIANA SEMI-SWEET MUSCADINE TABLE WINE

GROWN, PRODUCED AND BOTTLED BY FELICIANA CELLARS WINERY & VINEYARDS, LTD. JACKSON, LOUISIANA

MAINE

As Maine is known more for blueberries than grapes, most of the state's winemakers decided to feature blueberry wine when they found it too cold to grow traditional wine grapes.

—B.S.E.

STATE WEB SITE: www.americanwineries.org

NUMBER OF WINERIES: 7

U.S. RANK FOR NUMBER OF BONDED WINERIES: #36

FIRST WINERY: Bartlett Maine Estate Winery, 1982

LARGEST WINERY: Bartlett Maine Estate Winery (fruits); Cellar Door Winery (grapes)

WELL-KNOWN WINERIES: Bartlett Maine Estate Winery, Blacksmiths Winery, Cellar Door Winery, Winterport Winery

AMERICAN VITICULTURAL AREAS: none

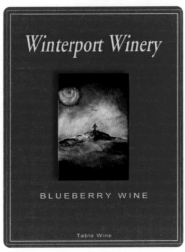

Cumberland Valley

Linganore

Catoctin

MARYLAND

"Growing Grapes for Wine," a program developed by the Southern Maryland Tri-County Council, began in 2005 in an effort to preserve land from development by using tobacco buy-out money to grow grapes. The money raised will assist farmers transitioning from tobacco crops to grapevines. The state of Maryland has viticulture initiatives ranging from a comprehensive Web site to government-funded programs.

—I.R.

STATE WEB SITE: www.marylandwine.com

NUMBER OF WINERIES: 16

U.S. RANK FOR NUMBER OF BONDED WINERIES: #29

MARYLAND
*M*ERLOT
Fermented and Bottled by Linganore Winecellars
Mount Airy, Maryland
ALC. BY VOL 12.5%

FIRST WINERY: Boordy Vineyards, 1945

LARGEST WINERY: Linganore Winecellars

WELL-KNOWN WINERIES: Boordy Vineyards, Catoctin Vineyards, Cygnus Wine Cellars, Elk Run Vineyards, Fiore Winery, Linganore Winecellars, Little Ashby Vineyards, Loew Vineyards

TOP GRAPES: Cabernet Sauvignon, Cabernet Franc, Merlot, Chardonnay, Petite Verdot, Chambourcin, Seyval, Vidal, Traminette

AMERICAN VITICULTURAL AREAS: 3—Catoctin, Cumberland Valley, Linganore

BOORDY
VINEYARDS

CHARDONNAY
MARYLAND

This fine Chardonnay is grown at our estate vineyards in the Long Green Valley and South Mountain. Fermentation in French oak barrels and aging on the yeast yields a rich flavor with delicate citrus and melon aromas. Serve with poultry, fish, and light meats. Less than 1000 cases produced.

Southeastern
New England

Martha's Vineyard

MASSACHUSETTS

Westport Rivers Winery pioneered growing grapes along the shores of Long Island Sound in Massachusetts; this is the mildest region of the state, in its southeastern corner. Inland, Nashoba Valley Winery chose to make a name for itself with a plethora of fruit-based wines. Most wineries here have chosen one or the other: either fruit or wine grapes. Every year another winery or two pops up, in locations ranging from near the New York border in the west to Cape Cod in the east.

—B.S.E.

STATE WEB SITE:
www.mass.gov/agr/massgrown/wineries.htm

NUMBER OF WINERIES: 15

U.S. RANK FOR NUMBER OF BONDED WINERIES: #30

FIRST WINERY: Chicāma, 1973

LARGEST WINERY: Westport Rivers Winery

WELL-KNOWN WINERIES: Nantucket Winery, Nashoba Valley Winery, Westport Rivers Winery

TOP GRAPES: Chardonnay, Pinot Noir, Riesling, Gewürztraminer, Pinot Blanc, Pinot Gris, Cayuga, Vidal Blanc

AMERICAN VITICULTURAL AREAS: 2—Martha's Vineyard, Southeastern New England

WINE TRAILS:
Coastal Wine Trail

CUVÉE RJR
Southeastern New England
TRADITIONAL METHOD SPARKLING WINE

GROWN, PRODUCED AND BOTTLED BY
WESTPORT RIVERS WINERY, WESTPORT, MASSACHUSETTS

ALCOHOL 12% BY VOLUME

CHICĀMA
VINEYARDS

Martha's Vineyard
Viognier

Estate Bottled

West Tisbury, Martha's Vineyard, Massachusetts
ALCOHOL 11.5% BY VOLUME

Leelanau Peninsula /
Old Mission Peninsula

Lake Michigan Shore / Fennville

MICHIGAN

As with other states bordering the Great Lakes to the
east, Michigan's grape industry is dominated by
Concord, Niagara, and other native varieties. However, due to the state's geography and the lake effect
phenomenon, *vinifera* viticulture is possible in two
zones: the extreme southwest (encompassing the
Michigan Shore and Fennville AVAs), and two
peninsulas around Traverse Bay in the northwest
(the Leelanau Peninsula and Old Mission Peninsula
AVAs). The prevailing westerly winds crossing Lake
Michigan and the moderating effect of the lake create pockets of temperate climate, allowing for fruit
cultivation including the classic cool-climate European grape varieties. Without the moderating lake
effect, only native and hardy French hybrid varieties
would grow there. The westerly winds delay bud-
break in the spring until the risk of frost is largely
past and extend the length of the growing season in
the fall.

The best of Michigan's wines are among the finest
in the country, demonstrating classic cool-climate
character similar to that found in New York's Finger
Lakes region where *vinifera* varieties can also be cultivated for similar reasons. In 2000, a sparkling
cuvée from L. Mawby won Best Sparkling Wine in
the International Eastern Wine Competition, and in
2003, a semidry Riesling from Peninsula Cellars
won Riesling Champion in that same competition.
Riesling, Pinot Gris, Gewürztraminer, and Cabernet

Franc are star *vinifera* varieties (respectable but not stellar Pinot Noir has been made from Dijon clones), and sparkling wine has long been a stylistic specialty in the state. Hybrid varieties also make fine wine, from Vidal Blanc, Vignoles, and Chancellor.

Fruit cultivation has a long history in Michigan, which is noted for the quality of its cherries. Many Michigan wineries make products from cherries, ranging from cherry wine to oak-aged award-winning ports, to *eaux de vie*. Michigan in fact is a leader in regional fruit brandy production, and many fruit farmers have survived thanks to the prices offered by wineries such as Black Star Farms, making three levels of pear brandy, and by growing the Williams pear inside bottles tied on the tree, in the European tradition.

After a protracted battle, in 2005, Michigan vintners finally won the right to ship limited quantities of wine direct to consumers. Wine tourism is so important to the industry that David Creighton, marketing specialist for the industry, notes that word-of-mouth is as important as commercial marketing. In addition, the state tourism office has now recognized the importance of winery tourism and has added a significant wine component to their out-of-state marketing targeted at nearby Illinois, Indiana, and Ohio.

—R.L.

(continued)

SHADY LANE

PINOT NOIR
LEELANAU PENINSULA

ALC. 12% BY VOL./ 750ML

CHÂTEAU
GRAND
TRAVERSE
LATE HARVEST
JOHANNISBERG RIESLING

ALCOHOL 10.5% BY VOLUME

State Web site: www.michiganwines.com

Number of wineries: 73

U.S. rank for number of bonded wineries: #9

First winery: St. Julian Wine Co., 1921

Largest winery: St. Julian Wine Co.

Well-known wineries: Chateau Chantal, Château Grand Traverse, Fenn Valley, L. Mawby Vineyards, Peninsula Cellars, St. Julian, Tabor Hill, Winery at Black Star Farms

Top grapes: Riesling, Gewürztraminer, Pinot Gris/Pinot Grigio, Vidal Blanc, Cabernet Franc, Concord, Niagara

American viticultural areas: 4—Fennville, Lake Michigan Shore, Leelanau Peninsula, Old Mission Peninsula

Wine trails: Southeast Michigan Pioneer Wine Trail, Southwest Michigan Wine Trail, Wineries of Old Mission Peninsula, Leelanau Peninsula Vintners

Best bets: 2004, 2005

MINNESOTA

The late Minnesota wine pioneer David Bailly tried to show the potential for fine wine grown in the Northstar State by reminding people that great wines come from marginal sites. Displayed prominently under the state name on the label, Bailly printed his winery's slogan, "Where the grapes can suffer." Garrison Keillor once made a humorous comment about a Minnesota Chardonnay during a "Lives of the Cowboys" sketch on the *Prairie Home Companion* radio show, calling Minnesota winemaking an oxymoron. A sensitive grower who actually grew the variety in Minnesota took offense at the comment. The wine producer had buried the vines each winter to keep them alive, but eventually had to surrender to winter.

Despite legendary low winter temperatures and a large Nordic population for whom vine cultivation is not in their past, Minnesota not only has a thriving wine industry today but has made important contributions to American viticulture through the grape-breeding program at the University of Minnesota. A Wisconsin dairyman and grape-breeding hobbyist, Elmer Swenson became so successful hybridizing new hardy and high-quality varieties that

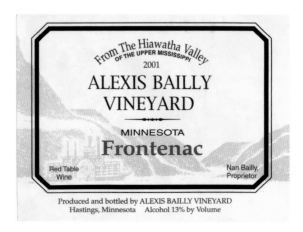

From The Hiawatha Valley
OF THE UPPER MISSISSIPPI
2001

ALEXIS BAILLY VINEYARD

MINNESOTA

Frontenac

Red Table Wine

Nan Bailly, Proprietor

Produced and bottled by ALEXIS BAILLY VINEYARD
Hastings, Minnesota   Alcohol 13% by Volume

he was invited to carry on his research at the university. His cold-hardy hybrids like Swenson's Red and La Crosse produced wine superior to most of the parent hybrids and have been planted in seventeen states and a half-dozen foreign countries. The university carries on his work, and the most promising new generation of cold-hardy, high-quality red hybrid Frontenac was released in 1996, followed by Frontenac Gris, La Crescent, and Marquette. These hybrids are responsible for the rapid growth of Minnesota viticulture to its current five hundred acres, fast replacing the old French hybrids and giving the state's wine industry a promising future.

—R.L.

STATE WEB SITE: www.mngrapes.org

NUMBER OF WINERIES: 17

U.S. RANK FOR NUMBER OF BONDED WINERIES: #27

FIRST WINERY: Alexis Bailly Vineyard, 1976

LARGEST WINERY: Carlos Creek Vineyards

WELL-KNOWN WINERIES: Alexis Bailly Vineyard, St. Croix Vineyards, Wine Haven

TOP GRAPES: Frontenac, Frontenac Gris, La Crescent, Marquette, St. Croix, Prairie Star

AMERICAN VITICULTURAL AREA: 1—Alexandria Lakes

WINE TRAILS: Three Rivers Wine Trail

MISSISSIPPI

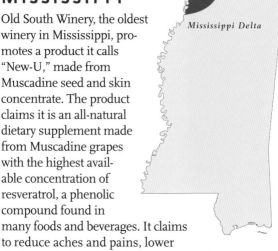

Mississippi Delta

Old South Winery, the oldest winery in Mississippi, promotes a product it calls "New-U," made from Muscadine seed and skin concentrate. The product claims it is an all-natural dietary supplement made from Muscadine grapes with the highest available concentration of resveratrol, a phenolic compound found in many foods and beverages. It claims to reduce aches and pains, lower cholesterol, slow the aging process, and inhibit the growth of cancer. Who knew that you could prolong life just by taking a vitamin made from Muscadine?

—I.R.

STATE WEB SITE: www.americanwineries.org

NUMBER OF WINERIES: 4

U.S. RANK FOR NUMBER OF BONDED WINERIES: #46

FIRST WINERY: Old South Winery, 1979

LARGEST WINERY: Old South Winery

WELL-KNOWN WINERIES: Gulf Coast Winery, Old South Winery

TOP GRAPE: Muscadine

AMERICAN VITICULTURAL AREA: 1— Mississippi Delta

Old South

Miss Scarlett
Sweet Muscadine Table Wine
Mississippi Native Wine

MISSOURI

The history of grape growing and winemaking in Missouri dates to 1837, when German immigrants began planting grapes near St. Louis. By the late nineteenth century, Missouri was producing some of the best wines in the United States. The first American Viticultural Area in the U.S. was Augusta, Missouri, designated in 1980. Since then, the wine growing regions of Ozark Highlands, Ozark Mountain, and Hermann have also been designed AVAs. Stone Hill Winery is one of the top tourist attractions in the state with its two locations.

—I.R.

STATE WEB SITE: www.missouriwine.org

NUMBER OF WINERIES: 66

U.S. RANK FOR NUMBER OF BONDED WINERIES: #10

FIRST WINERY: Stone Hill Winery, 1847

LARGEST WINERY: St. James Winery

WELL-KNOWN WINERIES: Augusta Vineyards, Les Bourgeois Winery & Vineyards, Montelle Winery, Stone Hill Winery

TOP GRAPES: Cynthiana/Norton, Vignoles, Seyval Blanc, Chambourcin, Chardonel, Vidal Blanc

AMERICAN VITICULTURAL AREAS:
4—Augusta, Hermann, Ozark Highlands, Ozark Mountain

Montana

Ten Spoon Vineyard & Winery is the new name Andy Sponseller and partner Connie Potten gave their winery after a trademark challenge convinced them they could not continue to operate under the name of Rattlesnake Creek Vineyard. Their new name is the result of a contest they conducted, offering a free case of wine for life to the winner. They received some thousand entries, and after checking for trademark issues among the ten finalists, chose the name that is, sort of, a combination of their two last names. The winning entry came from a wine expert at one of Denmark's largest wholesalers.

—S.T.

State Web site: www.americanwineries.org

Number of wineries: 9

U.S. rank for number of bonded wineries: #34

First winery: Mission Mountain Winery, 1984

Largest winery: Lolo Peak Winery

Well-known wineries: Clear Weather, Lolo Peak Winery, Ten Spoon Vineyard & Winery

Top grapes: Maréchal Foch, Frontenac, Leon Millot, and St. Croix

American viticultural areas: none

RATTLESNAKE CREEK

FAT CAT

spike

organic
montana white wine

ALC 12.5% BY VOL.   750 ML

Nebraska

Ed Swanson opened his Cuthills Vineyards winery in northeast Nebraska in 1994, but he'd already planted most of his vineyards by 1985. He makes all of his wines from Nebraska-grown grapes (and honey). His plantings are mostly French hybrids, but also many experimental varieties as he—like his Nebraska winemaking colleagues—keeps looking for the perfect match of grapes and terroir.

—S.T.

STATE WEB SITE: www.nebraskawines.com

NUMBER OF WINERIES: 13

U.S. RANK FOR NUMBER OF BONDED WINERIES: #31

FIRST WINERY: Cuthills Vineyards, 1994

LARGEST WINERY: James Arthur Vineyards

WELL-KNOWN WINERIES:
Cuthills Vineyards, James Arthur Vineyards

TOP GRAPES:
LaCrosse, Edelweiss, St. Croix, Maréchal Foch, and Seyval Blanc

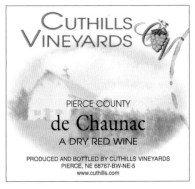

AMERICAN VITICULTURAL AREAS:
none

NEVADA

Tahoe Ridge Winery has invested many years to determine which grapes grow best in their northern Nevada location. They have concluded that many of the *Vitis vinifera* grapes are too expensive to grow there, especially considering that their neighboring state, California, is one of the world's great wine-growing regions. So, for the time being, much of the winery's production will depend on purchasing California grapes, but the winemakers are determined to work with Nevada growers to find the best grapes for Nevada and to make wines distinctive to their state.

—S.T.

STATE WEB SITE: www.americanwineries.org

NUMBER OF WINERIES: 4

U.S. RANK FOR NUMBER OF BONDED WINERIES: #47

FIRST WINERY: Pahrump Valley Winery, 1990

LARGEST WINERY: Pahrump Valley Winery

WELL-KNOWN WINERIES:
Pahrump Valley Winery, Tahoe Ridge Vineyards

TOP GRAPES: Cabernet Sauvignon, Merlot, Chardonnay

AMERICAN VITICULTURAL AREAS: none

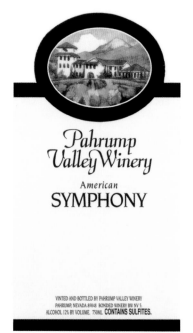

Pahrump Valley Winery

American
SYMPHONY

VINTED AND BOTTLED BY PAHRUMP VALLEY WINERY
PAHRUMP, NEVADA 89048 BONDED WINERY BW NV 5.
ALCOHOL 12% BY VOLUME. 750ML. **CONTAINS SULFITES.**

New Hampshire

Somehow there is a tiny grape-growing microclimate on the border of New Hampshire and Massachusetts, as the owners of Jewell Town Vineyards discovered twenty-five years ago. With more recent hybrid grape development, several new wineries are expected to begin planting and producing wines in other areas of the state during the next few years—though some will also produce fruit wines.

—B.S.E.

State Web site: www.americanwineries.org

Number of wineries: 6

U.S. rank for number of bonded wineries: #42

First winery: Jewell Towne Vineyards, 1994

Largest winery: Flag Hill Winery

Well-known wineries: Flag Hill Winery, Jewell Towne Vineyards

Top grapes: Leon Millot, Maréchal Foch, Seyval Blanc, Vidal Blanc

American viticultural areas: none

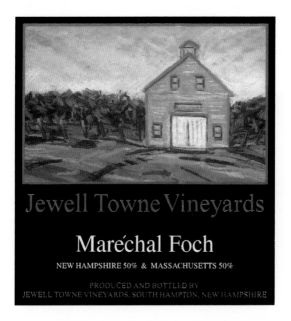

Jewell Towne Vineyards

Maréchal Foch

NEW HAMPSHIRE 50% & MASSACHUSETTS 50%

PRODUCED AND BOTTLED BY
JEWELL TOWNE VINEYARDS, SOUTH HAMPTON, NEW HAMPSHIRE

NEW JERSEY

New Jersey is one of the few eastern states with a winery still in operation from the mid-nineteenth century, the Renault Winery in Egg Harbor. The Renault Winery became known for its Charmat-process sparkling wines and wines made from the native white Noah grape. Today it is chiefly known for its sparkling blueberry wines. Another legacy of New Jersey viticultural history is the town of Vineland, in Cumberland County, where the Delaware grape was discovered in 1894, and where a teetotaller dentist by the name of Dr. Welch discovered how to sterilize Concord juice for Communion by Methodist and other churches. "Dr. Welch's Grape Juice" spread from churches to drugstore sales, and sparked the national Concord grape and juice industry. An important legacy of Dr. Welch's discovery is the Royal Kedem Wine Company, located since 2001 in Bayonne, the largest producer, importer, and distributor of kosher-certified wines in the world.

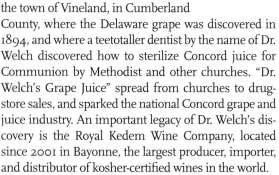

Farm winery legislation in 1982 allowed for the renaissance of the state wine industry. New Jersey wineries tend to be clustered in two groups. The first is the northwestern group (north of a line running from Trenton to Raritan Bay), many in the Delaware

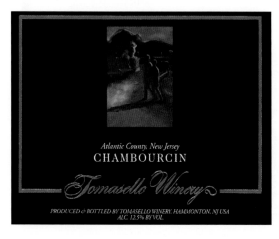

Atlantic County, New Jersey
CHAMBOURCIN
Tomasello Winery
PRODUCED & BOTTLED BY TOMASELLO WINERY, HAMMONTON, NJ USA
ALC. 12.5% BY VOL.

River Valley; and the second is clustered in south-central New Jersey near Hammonton.

Quality Riesling is grown in the cooler locations, while red Bordeaux varieties perform well in warmer sites. Unionville Vineyards has produced fine *vinifera* wines and won a double gold in the International Eastern Wine Competition for a 2002 Meritage-style Hunter's Red Reserve. New Jersey also produces superior fruit wines, with Cream Ridge Winery leading the way with an oak-aged Montmorenci cherry wine (called ciliegia amabile, or "lovable cherry") that consistently wins the top award in the state for fruit wines. New Jersey is a leading producer of blueberries, and many wineries besides Renault make blueberry wines.

—R.L.

STATE WEB SITE: www.newjerseywines.com

NUMBER OF WINERIES: 32

U.S. RANK FOR NUMBER OF BONDED WINERIES: #15

FIRST WINERY: Renault Winery, 1861

LARGEST WINERY: Royal Kedem Wine Co.

WELL-KNOWN WINERIES: Alba Vineyard, Cream Ridge Winery, Tomasello Winery, Unionville Vineyards, Valenzano Winery

TOP GRAPES: Riesling, Chardonnay, Cabernet Franc, Merlot, Cabernet Sauvignon, Pinot Gris, Viognier, Chambourcin, Vidal Blanc

AMERICAN VITICULTURAL AREAS: 2—Central Delaware Valley, Warren Hills

WINE TRAILS: Coastal Wine Trail, Delaware Wine Trail, East/West Wine Trail, Hunterdon County Wine Trail, Mid-State Wine Trails A and B, Northwest Wine Trail, South Wine Trail, South Central Wine Trails A and B, Southeast Wine Trail, Southernmost Wine Trail

Mesilla Valley

Middle Rio Grande Valley

Mimbres Valley

NEW MEXICO

When the Gruet family from France's Champagne region looked to start a winery in the United States, they found the right growing conditions and the right price in New Mexico. The success of their highly acclaimed sparkling wines, created by the traditional methods of their native Champagne, is one factor in the growing recognition of the good quality wines being produced in New Mexico.

—S.T.

14.3% Alcohol by Vol.   375 ML

Dessert Wine
Gewürztraminer
New Mexico
Estate   Bottled

Casa Rondeña
Winery
Los Ranchos Vineyard
Vinted & Bottled
by John R. Calvin

STATE WEB SITE: www.nmwine.com

NUMBER OF WINERIES: 28

U.S. RANK FOR NUMBER OF BONDED WINERIES: #18

FIRST WINERY: La Vina Winery, 1977

LARGEST WINERY: St. Clair Winery

WELL-KNOWN WINERIES: Casa Rondeña Winery, Gruet Winery, La Chiripada, Milagro Vineyards

TOP GRAPES: Cabernet Sauvignon, Chardonnay, Johannisberg Riesling, Merlot, Pinot Noir, Sauvignon Blanc, Zinfandel

AMERICAN VITICULTURAL AREAS: 4—Mesilla Valley, Middle Rio Grande Valley, Mimbres Valley, Rio Grande Valley

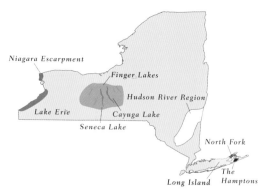

Niagara Escarpment
Finger Lakes
Hudson River Region
Lake Erie
Cayuga Lake
Seneca Lake
North Fork
The
Long Island Hamptons

NEW YORK

New York is my home state. I began my study of wine, grape growing, and winemaking more than thirty years ago, first in the Hudson Valley and then in the Finger Lakes district. (Back then there were no wineries on Long Island.) I'm extremely pleased with the progress in making quality world-class wines in New York. It's been an exciting ride. I'm now a grape grower and soon to be a winery owner in New York.

See Chapter 5 for more information on New York wines and winemaking.

—K.Z.

STATE WEB SITE: www.newyorkwines.org

NUMBER OF WINERIES: 210

U.S. RANK FOR NUMBER OF BONDED WINERIES: #4

FIRST WINERY: Brotherhood Winery, 1839

Dr. Konstantin Frank

NEW YORK
Johannisberg Riesling

DRY

ALC 11.5% VOL

LARGEST WINERY: Canandaigua Wine Company

WELL-KNOWN WINERIES: See Chapter 5

AMERICAN VITICULTURAL AREAS:
9—Cayuga Lake
Finger Lakes
The Hamptons
Hudson River Region
Lake Erie
Long Island
Niagara Escarpment
North Fork of Long Island
Seneca Lake

(continued)

ACRES OF VINES:
31,000 +

U.S. RANK FOR ACRES OF VINES:
#2

TOP GRAPES:
Merlot
Cabernet Franc
Riesling
Chardonnay
Cabernet
  Sauvignon
Pinot Noir

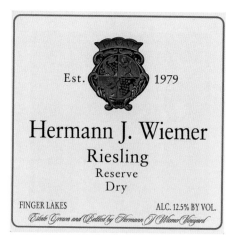

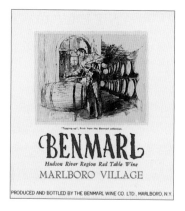

MILLBROOK

PINOT NOIR
NEW YORK STATE

PRODUCED AND BOTTLED BY MILLBROOK WINERY, INC., MILLBROOK, N.Y. 12545 750 ML 13% ALC. BY VOL.

Wölffer®

The Hamptons, Long Island
LATE HARVEST
CHARDONNAY

ESTATE BOTTLED BY WÖLFFER ESTATE
SAGAPONACK, NEW YORK, USA • ALC. 8.70% BY VOL. • 375 ML

LENZ

OLD VINES
MERLOT

NORTH FORK OF LONG ISLAND

UNFILTERED

Yadkin Valley

NORTH CAROLINA

In North Carolina, tobacco farmers are looking to grapes for their continued livelihood. Winemakers from New York, Washington State, Ohio, and other faraway places are coming to North Carolina to be a part of the action.

North Carolina's largest winery, Biltmore Estate, in Asheville, is one of the most visited wineries in the United States.

Shelton Vineyards, a major player in making Yadkin Valley North Carolina's first AVA, hosts a magnificent winery as well as a quaint restaurant surrounded by Riesling, Cabernet Franc, and Syrah vines. NASCAR magnate Richard Childress and partner Greg Johns own Childress Vineyards, relatively new to the valley but already a popular travel destination. The valley is also home to Westbend Vineyards, the oldest vineyard and first bonded winery in the area, and Rag Apple Lassie Vineyards, one of only a few wineries on the East Coast to grow Zinfandel.

There is speculation that Swan Creek will receive AVA status. Located within the Yadkin Valley AVA, Swan Creek is spread across Wilkes, Yadkin, and Iredell counties.

Wine consumers can find great wines throughout the state—in Burlington, Charlotte, Greensboro, Mount Airy, and off I-40 near the Raleigh-Durham Airport, where Chatham Hill Winery makes wine in a concrete warehouse.

—I.R.

State Web site: www.ncwine.org

Number of wineries: 49

U.S. rank for number of bonded wineries: #13

First winery: Medoc Vineyard, 1835

Largest winery: Biltmore Estate

(continued)

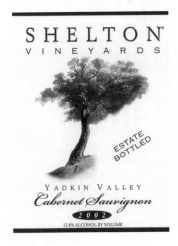

WELL-KNOWN WINERIES: Biltmore Estate, Chatham Hill Winery, Childress Vineyards, RagApple Lassie Vineyards, RayLen Vineyards, Rock House Vineyards, Shelton Vineyards, Westbend Vineyards

TOP GRAPES: Scuppernong, Chardonnay, Cabernet Sauvignon, Merlot, Viognier, Cabernet Franc

AMERICAN VITICULTURAL AREA: 1—Yadkin Valley

WINE TRAILS: Haw River Wine Trail, Swan Creek Wine Trail, Yadkin Valley Wine Trail

BEST BETS: 2002, 2004, 2005, 2006

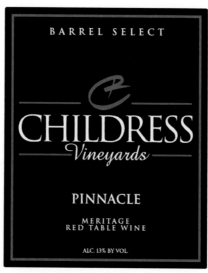

North Dakota

When the Pointe of View Winery began operating in 2002, it made North Dakota the fiftieth and final state to have a winery and marked the first time in American history that there is at least one winery in each of the fifty states.

—S.T.

State Web site: www.ndgga.org

Number of wineries: 4

U.S. rank for number of bonded wineries: #48

First winery: Pointe of View Winery, 2002

Largest winery: Pointe of View Winery

Well-known wineries: Maple River Winery, Pointe of View Winery

Top grapes: Frontenac, Prairie Star

American viticultural areas: none

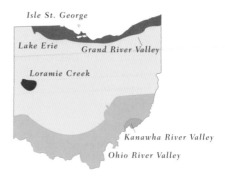

Isle St. George

Lake Erie   Grand River Valley

Loramie Creek

Kanawha River Valley

Ohio River Valley

OHIO

By 1859, Ohio was the premier wine-producing state in the nation, thanks to three thousand acres of Catawba vineyards near Cincinnati in the Ohio River Valley, with a third of the national total and more than twice as much as California. The American poet Longfellow was so impressed with the wine, he wrote "Ode to Catawba Wine." However, Catawba is vulnerable to powdery mildew, also known as oïdium. A blight broke out that wiped out the Ohio River vineyards in the 1860s.

These vineyards were soon replaced by new plantings along Lake Erie from Toledo to Cleveland, where cool lake breezes kept disease pressure low, and the industry grew larger than before, only to be stymied by Prohibition.

Today, the Ohio wine industry is one of the most diverse in the East, with wines from native labrusca varieties like Concord and Catawba, along with French hybrids, and fine *vinifera* wines. Most of the state's 2,500 acres of grapes are, in fact, Concord and Niagara, as is common with grape-growing states along the Great Lakes, but *vinifera* varieties are the fastest-growing category. Meier's Wine Cellars, a remnant of the boom days of the nineteenth century, is the state's largest winery (a division of Paramount Distillers). Each year Meier's produces nearly three million gallons of branded wine sold throughout the country.

Ohio has six AVAs, most either along the Lake Erie shore in the north or in the Ohio River Valley. French hybrids like Vidal Blanc and Chambourcin are strong, and the best *vinifera* wines range from Riesling, Pinot Gris, and Chardonnay in the cool northern AVAs to Cabernet Sauvignon and Cabernet Franc in the Ohio River Valley. One of the smallest but most distinctive AVAs in the country is the Isle St. George, surrounded by Lake Erie. It contains one of the largest plantings of *vinifera* grapes in the state, and the moderating maritime influence extends the growing season to the longest in the northeastern United States, with harvest as late as six weeks following that in other nearby regions.

Despite the established potential for high-quality dry *vinifera*, the average Ohio palate prefers sweeter styles, and few Ohio wines are completely dry. Ohio produces high-quality dessert wines from Vidal Blanc. In 2005, Ferrante Vineyards won two double golds in the International Eastern Wine Competition (IEWC) for a late-harvest and ice-wine Vidal, both from 2003. Fruit wines are popular, and some of the best fruit wines in the East are from Ohio. The Winery at Versailles and Maize Valley Winery both won Best Fruit Wine in recent International Eastern Wine Competitions; other double gold Ohio wines in IEWC recently include Breitenbach's Road House Red and Ferrante's 2004 Riesling (Best Semidry Riesling in 2006). Winery tourism is strong in Ohio, and the annual Vintage Ohio Wine Festival, produced by the Ohio Wine Producers Association, draws tens of thousands to Metroparks Farmpark in Kirtland (Lake County) the first weekend of August.

—R.L.

(continued)

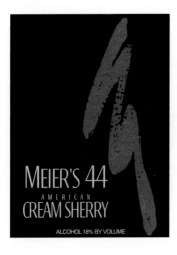

STATE WEB SITE: www.ohiowines.org

NUMBER OF WINERIES: 92

U.S. RANK FOR NUMBER OF BONDED WINERIES: #7

FIRST WINERY: Meier's Wine Cellars, 1890

LARGEST WINERY: Meier's Wine Cellars

WELL-KNOWN WINERIES:
Breitenbach Wine Cellars, Chalet Debonné, Ferrante Winery, Firelands, Kinkead Ridge Maize Valley Winery, Markko Vineyards, Mon Ami Wine Co., St. Joseph Winery, Winery at Versailles

TOP GRAPES:
Riesling, Pinot Gris, Chardonnay, Vidal Blanc, Cabernet Sauvignon, Cabernet Franc, Chambourcin, Concord, Niagara, Catawba

AMERICAN VITICULTURAL AREAS:
6—Grand River Valley, Isle St. George, Kanawha River Valley, Lake Erie, Loramie Creek, Ohio River Valley

WINE TRAILS:
Wing Watch and Wine Trail, Wines & Vines Wine Trail, Capital City Wine Trail, Canal Country Wine Trail, Appalachian Heritage Wine Trail, Nicolas Longworth Heritage Wine Trail

BEST BETS:
2002, 2005

Ozark Mountain

OKLAHOMA

Tidal School Vineyards derives its name from the historic building that now houses the winery. Built in 1929 by John D. Rockefeller, and later purchased by J. Paul Getty as a school for the children of his Tidewater Oil Co. employees, the building needed restoration estimated at $500,000, but a lot of people donated their work. According to newspaper reports, one contractor said he'd rather have stock than payment. He may have been onto something: In 2000 there were only two wineries in Oklahoma.

—S.T.

STATE WEB SITE: www.oklahomawines.org

NUMBER OF WINERIES: 27

U.S. RANK FOR NUMBER OF BONDED WINERIES: #19

FIRST WINERY: Cimarron Cellars, 1983

LARGEST WINERY: Tidal School Vineyards

WELL-KNOWN WINERIES: Stone Bluff Cellars, Tidal School Vineyards

TOP GRAPES: Cynthiana, Vignoles, Chardonnay, Shiraz, Zinfandel, Riesling

AMERICAN VITICULTURAL AREA: 1—Ozark Mountain

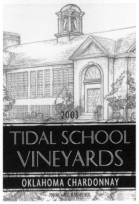

OREGON

Even though Oregon is fourth in production of wine in the United States, most of the wineries are small, family-owned, artisanal producers. The passion for winemaking is evident especially with the great Pinot Noir wines. For the "wine trailblazers," the accessibility and convenience of the wineries from the city of Portland and its beautiful coast makes this a "must visit" wine region. For more information on Oregon wines and winemaking, see Chapter 5.

—K.Z.

State Web site: www.oregonwine.org

Number of wineries: 230

U.S. rank for number of bonded wineries: #3

First winery: Hillcrest Vineyards, 1961

Largest winery: Willamette Valley Vineyards

(continued)

WELL-KNOWN WINERIES: See Chapter 5

AMERICAN VITICULTURAL AREAS: 14—Applegate Valley, Columbia Gorge, Columbia Valley, Dundee Hills, Eola-Amity Hills, McMinnville, Red Hill Douglas County, Ribbon Ridge, Rogue Valley, Southern Oregon, Umpqua Valley, Walla Walla Valley, Willamette Valley, Yamhill-Carlton District

ACRES OF VINES: 11,300 +

U.S. RANK FOR ACRES OF VINES: #5

TOP GRAPES: Chardonnay, Pinot Gris, Pinot Noir

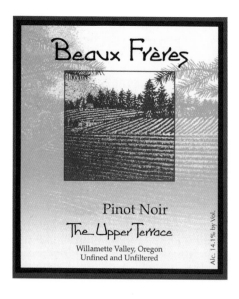

Knudsen Erath

Dundee Villages

OREGON
PINOT NOIR

PRODUCED AND BOTTLED BY
KNUDSEN ERATH WINERY, DUNDEE, OREGON, USA OR BW-OR-52
ALC 13% BY VOL.

REX HILL

OREGON
PINOT NOIR

RESERVE

The Eyrie Vineyards

Oregon Pinot gris

WILLAMETTE VALLEY
ESTATE GROWN

ALCOHOL
13% BY VOL.

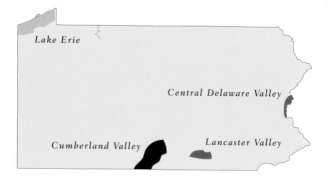

Lake Erie

Central Delaware Valley

Cumberland Valley

Lancaster Valley

PENNSYLVANIA

Pennsylvania has a wine history dating to the seventeenth century. Colony founder William Penn brought French and Spanish vines to the Philadelphia area in 1683, which failed like similar attempts in Jamestown and elsewhere in the East. But the first commercial wine industry in the United States took hold in Pennsylvania, with centers around Pittsburgh and York in the early nineteenth century, based on the Alexander grape and native varieties.

The Keystone State made an important contribution to the American wine industry through its pioneering Farm Winery Act in 1968, which established small family farm wineries and vineyards as legally (and for tax purposes) distinct from large commercial wineries, and which has been used as a model for dozens of other states. Much of the credit for this important work goes to Doug Moorhead of Presque Isle Wine Cellars in the northeast, on Lake Erie. Prior to this legislation, the first post-Prohibition vintner in the state, Melvin Gordon of the now-defunct Conestoga Vineyard, could not serve his own wine without buying it back from the Pennsylvania Liquor Control Board.

While Pennsylvania boasts some fourteen thousand acres of grapevines, almost 90 percent of them are planted on the Lake Erie shore and are mostly Concord and Niagara, which are used for juice production. Eighteen hundred acres are planted with

CHADDSFORD

Pinot Noir

BARREL SELECT

wine grapes, both French hybrid and *vinifera* varieties. While there are several AVAs in Pennsylvania, most wineries are clustered in the warm and populous southeastern quadrant of the state, between the Blue Mountains, Maryland state line, and Delaware River, with Philadelphia and Amish country in the Lancaster Valley serving as important magnets for winery tourism. The Chesapeake Bay has a moderating maritime effect, and fruit trees are cultivated in the region. Some bold vintners like Christian Klay

(continued)

(Christian W. Klay Winery) have vineyards in the Allegheny Mountains, but site and selection of varieties are crucial. Klay's vineyards face southwest for warmth and protection from cold winds.

Chaddsford, the largest winery in Pennsylvania, deftly produces a range of fine *vinifera* ranging from Pinot Grigio to a proprietary Meritage-style blend, and also one of the best Chambourcins in the state. Fine Pinot Grigio is made by the Winery at Wilcox, and impressive Merlot by Blue Mountain Vineyards. Recent Pennsylvania winners of double gold medals in the International Eastern Wine Competition include Clover Hill (for Catawba) and Nissley (for apple); the Winery at Wilcox won Best Fruit Wine in 2004 for a sparkling blueberry wine.

Pennsylvania hosts Wineries Unlimited, the largest wine trade conference in the East, which takes place annually at the Valley Forge Convention Center in mid-March.

—R.L.

STATE WEB SITE: www.pennsylvaniawine.com

NUMBER OF WINERIES: 99

U.S. RANK FOR NUMBER OF BONDED WINERIES: #6

FIRST WINERY: Presque Isle Wine Cellars, 1964

LARGEST WINERY: Chaddsford Winery

WELL-KNOWN WINERIES: Adams County Winery, Blue Mountain Vineyards, Chaddsford Winery, Clover Hill Vineyard & Winery, Crossing Vineyard, Flickerwood Wine Cellars, Naylor Vineyards, Nissley Vineyards, Shade Mountain Vineyards, Sorrenti Cherry Valley Vineyards, Winery at Wilcox

TOP GRAPES: Cabernet Sauvignon, Cabernet Franc, Merlot, Chardonnay, Pinot Gris, Viognier, Vidal Blanc, Seyval Blanc, Chambourcin, Traminette, Concord, Niagara

AMERICAN VITICULTURAL AREAS: 4—Central Delaware Valley, Cumberland Valley, Lake Erie, Lancaster Valley

WINE TRAILS: Berks County Wine Trail, Mason Dixon Wine Trail, Uncork York Wine Trail, Brandywine Valley Wine Trail, Bucks County Wine Trail, Lehigh Valley Wine Trail, Chautauqua/Lake Erie Wine Trail, Groundhog Wine Trail, Susquehanna Heartland Wine Trail, Laurel Highlands Wine Trail, Sullivan County Wine Trail

BEST BETS: 2004, 2005

RHODE ISLAND

Sakonnet Vineyards has been credited with spearheading the New England wine movement in the 1970s; it was the first to take advantage of the mild influence of the coastline along the western shore of Long Island Sound. Several other wineries have followed, and they have all joined forces to create a new, picturesque wine trail through Rhode Island and into southeastern Massachusetts.

Southeaster New Englar

—B.S.E.

STATE WEB SITE: www.americanwineries.org

NUMBER OF WINERIES: 7

U.S. RANK FOR NUMBER OF BONDED WINERIES: #37

FIRST WINERY: Sakonnet Vineyards, 1975

LARGEST WINERY: Newport Vineyards & Winery

WELL-KNOWN WINERIES: Greenvale Vineyards, Newport Vineyards & Winery, Sakonnet Vineyards

TOP GRAPES: Chardonnay, Cabernet Franc, Gewürztraminer, Seyval Blanc, Vidal Blanc

AMERICAN VITICULTURAL AREA: 1—Southeastern New England Growing Appellation (includes part of Connecticut, Massachusetts, and Rhode Island)

WINE TRAILS: Coastal Wine Trails

SOUTH CAROLINA

South Carolina's wineries are sprinkled all over the state, from Myrtle Beach, Hilton Head, and Charleston, to Wadmalaw Island and Aiken. Though hurricanes are a major factor in the grape harvest statewide, wineries are still thriving, producing wines from Muscadine, Cabernet Sauvignon, Chardonnay, and other fruits such as plums and elderberries.

—I.R.

STATE WEB SITE: www.americanwineries.org

NUMBER OF WINERIES: 5

U.S. RANK FOR NUMBER OF BONDED WINERIES: #44

FIRST WINERY: Carolina Vineyards, formerly Cruse Vineyards, 1985

LARGEST WINERY: Carolina Vineyards

WELL-KNOWN WINERIES: Carolina Vineyards, Montmorenci Vineyards

TOP GRAPES: Scuppernong, Chambourcin, Vidal Blanc

AMERICAN VITICULTURAL AREAS: none

South Dakota

Valiant Vineyards has had some success with an unusual wine: Their Wild Grape wine is made from the *Vitis riparia* species, which is native to North America but less well known than the other native species, *Vitis labrusca*. Valiant's Wild Grape wine has made it to Paris wine shops, New York restaurants, and into the pages of such national media as *Time* magazine.

—S.T.

State Web site: www.americanwineries.org

Number of wineries: 10

U.S. rank for number of bonded wineries: #33

First winery: Valiant Vineyards Winery, 1996

Largest winery: Valiant Vineyards Winery

Well-known wineries: Prairie Berry Winery, Valiant Vineyards Winery

Top grapes: Baltica, Seyval Blanc, Maréchal Foch, Frontenac

American viticultural areas: none

South Dakota wines since 1876.

DEADWOOD

Fruit Table Wine
70% Black Currant &
30% Grape Wine

Prairie berry

SOUTH DAKOTA

Raspberry Honeywine

5% RASPBERRY WINE / 95% HONEYWINE
ALCOHOL 12% BY VOLUME

Prairie berry

PRODUCED & BOTTLED BY PRAIRIE BERRY, LLC, RAPID CITY, SOUTH DAKOTA

Mississippi Delta

TENNESSEE

Tennessee is one of a handful of American states that grow Nebbiolo, the Italian grape used to make Barbaresco and Barolo. In a very competitive wine market, Nebbiolo is a great grape to cultivate in the United States, where very little of this varietal is being grown. If Tennessee proves to be successful with this thin-skinned, finicky varietal, it could be the Piedmont of the South.

— I.R.

STATE WEB SITE: www.tennesseewines.com

NUMBER OF WINERIES: 24

U.S. RANK FOR NUMBER OF BONDED WINERIES: #22

FIRST WINERY: Highland Manor Winery, 1980

LARGEST WINERY: Mountain Valley Vineyards

WELL-KNOWN WINERIES: Beachaven Vineyards and Winery, Cordova Cellars

TOP GRAPES: Muscadine, Seyval Blanc, Chambourcin, Chardonnay, Nebbiolo

AMERICAN VITICULTURAL AREA: 1—Mississippi Delta

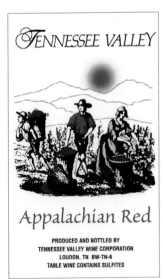

TENNESSEE VALLEY

Appalachian Red

PRODUCED AND BOTTLED BY
TENNESSEE VALLEY WINE CORPORATION
LOUDON, TN BW-TN-6
TABLE WINE CONTAINS SULFITES

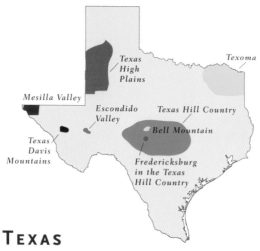

Texas
High
Plains

Texoma

Mesilla Valley

Escondido
Valley

Texas Hill Country

Bell Mountain

Texas
Davis
Mountains

Fredericksburg
in the Texas
Hill Country

TEXAS

The change in legislation allowing Texas wineries to
sell their wines to visitors has been a small step for
promoting winery tourism in the state. The wine industry took root in the 1970s when researchers
found that Texas's weather, soil, and climate are
ideal for growing grapes. It is now the fifth largest
wine-producing state behind only California, Oregon, Washington State, and New York.

—I.R.

VAL VERDE
WINERY

1883

FOUNDER
FRANK QUALIA

DON LUIS
Texas
TAWNY PORT

PROPRIETOR'S CHOICE § BLEND NO. 10
PRODUCED AND BOTTLED BY VAL VERDE WINERY
100 Qualia Dr., Del Rio, Tx. 78840 § Alcohol 18% by Volume

STATE WEB SITE: www.texaswine.com

NUMBER OF WINERIES: 89

U.S. RANK FOR NUMBER OF BONDED WINERIES: #8

FIRST WINERY: Val Verde Winery, 1883

LARGEST WINERY: St. Genevieve Winery

WELL-KNOWN WINERIES: Blue Mountain, Dry Comal Creek, Fall Creek, Flat Creek Estate, Llano Estacado, Lost Creek Vineyard and Winery, Quivis, Sister Creek Vineyards, Spicewood Vineyards

TOP GRAPES: Chenin Blanc, Chardonnay, Cabernet Sauvignon, Merlot

AMERICAN VITICULTURAL AREAS: 8—Bell Mountain, Escondido Valley, Fredericksburg, Mesilla Valley, Texas Davis Mountains, Texas High Plains, Texas Hill Country, Texoma

UTAH

Moab, Utah, with its breathtaking scenery (think Arches National Park) and spectacular outdoor recreation (think hiking, rafting, and slick-rock cycling), is a magnet for tourists from all over. Visitors can now add wine tasting to their activities, at the two wineries listed below. Both feature wines made from grapes grown locally, by the wineries and their neighbors.

—S.T.

STATE WEB SITE: www.americanwineries.org

NUMBER OF WINERIES: 7

U.S. RANK FOR NUMBER OF BONDED WINERIES: #38

FIRST WINERY: Castle Creek Winery, 1989

LARGEST WINERY: Castle Creek Winery

WELL-KNOWN WINERIES: Castle Creek Winery, Spanish Valley Vineyards & Winery

TOP GRAPES: Pinot Noir, Merlot, Cabernet Sauvignon, Chenin Blanc, Chardonnay, Gewürztraminer

AMERICAN VITICULTURAL AREAS: none

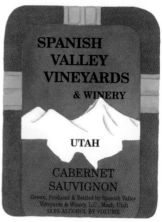

VERMONT

Large bodies of water can influence climate extremes, so it makes sense that Lake Champlain, on Vermont's western border, helps create a hospitable environment for grape growing in this state. Both there and in other areas of the state, several new wineries are expected to open in the next few years, due to plantings of hybrid grapes developed by agricultural programs at northern universities such as Minnesota and Cornell. Many of this state's wineries also make fruit wines; fruit and grape wine production are steadily increasing.

—B.S.E.

STATE WEB SITE: www.americanwineries.org

NUMBER OF WINERIES: 7

U.S. RANK FOR NUMBER OF BONDED WINERIES: #39

FIRST WINERY: Snow Farm Vineyard, 1998

LARGEST WINERY: Snow Farm Vineyard

WELL-KNOWN WINERIES: Boyden Valley Winery, Shelburne Vineyard, Snow Farm Vineyard and Winery

TOP GRAPES: Cayuga, Riesling, Vidal Blanc

AMERICAN VITICULTURAL AREAS: none

SNOW FARM VINEYARD

Vermont Seyval Blanc

n, produced and bottled
ow Farm Winery, LLC
Hero, Vermont

Table Wine
Contains sulfites
750 milliliters

Shelburne Vineyard

Riesling
Vermont Grown

Northern Neck
George Washington
Birthplace

Shenandoah
Valley

Monticello

North Fork of Roanoke

Rocky Knob

Eastern
Shore

VIRGINIA

From the start, Virginia was intent on establishing a serious wine industry. "Acte Twelve" of the Jamestown Assembly in 1619 required all male heads of household over age twenty to cultivate twenty imported *vinifera* grapevines "on pain of death" (commemorated in a Chardonnay named after the act produced by the Williamsburg Winery). Clearly the English investors of the Virginia Company were keen on ROI (return on investment, known at the time as "ye Quicke Buck"), but despite repeated efforts, ungrafted *vinifera* vines continued to fail, and tobacco was soon discovered as a more reliable cash crop. Patient efforts at viticulture continued in Virginia throughout the Colonial period, with no better example than Thomas Jefferson. The third president, with the aid of his friend Filipo Mazzei, brought Italian "vignerons" to plant Tuscan and other *vinifera* varieties at Monticello and nearby Colle, all in vain.

After twenty years, even the optimistic Jefferson conceded defeat. Putting his hopes on native varieties, he concluded prophetically, "We could, in the United States, make as great a variety of wines as are made in Europe, not exactly of the same kinds, but doubtless as good." In 1825, around the time of Jefferson's death, one Dr. Norton discovered a wild grape growing near Richmond; he cultivated it, made wine from it, and propagated it. Known first as Dr. Norton's Virginia Seedling, it is now known either as Cynthiana or Norton. Norton is of the *Vitis aestivalis* genus, and by 1873 the Monticello Wine Company was making a world-class "Virginia claret" based on local Norton.

Post-Prohibition, the Virginia wine industry revived in the late 1960s and has continued its growth to the present day as the second-largest wine producer in the East after New York. The industry made indifferent wines from French hybrids in the 1970s, began a shift to mainstream *vinifera* varieties in the 1980s, then diversified under the example of the iconoclastic Dennis Horton in the 1990s, who pioneered both Viognier and reintroduced Norton. Today, Virginia has one of the best quality and most diversified *vinifera* wine industries in the country, while still producing quality wines from hybrids Vidal Blanc, Seyval Blanc, Chambourcin, and Traminette. The *vinifera* range is clustered into mainstream international varietals (Chardonnay and the red Bordeaux varieties), Italian varieties (Pinot Grigio, Sangiovese, Malvasia, and Nebbiolo), and esoteric *vinifera* like Viognier, Touriga, Tannat, Tempranillo, Petit Manseng, and Albariño.

Wineries are spread throughout the state but are clustered in two major centers in the Upper Piedmont: Middleburg in Loudoun County, and Charlottesville in Albemarle County. Over time, the most consistent performance in top-quality wines seems to come from the latter, where the Monticello appellation encompasses the Upper Piedmont counties of Nelson, Albemarle, and Greene.

(continued)

2004
Viognier
Orange County, Virginia

HORTON

Stylistically, Virginia is between California and Europe (per its literal location), with fully ripe varietal character and rich New World flavors, but with restraint, elegance, and integration reminiscent of the Old World. Red Bordeaux blends are a core strength, in a Right Bank style with Cabernet Franc and Merlot dominant, and Petit Verdot as a successful regional specialty, the way Malbec is in Argentina. Chardonnay is also strong, with single vineyard bottlings from Ox Eye, Hardscrabble, and Meriwether vineyards revealing the complexity of terroir. Many observers (including California winemakers) acknowledged Viognier performs better in Virginia than anywhere else in the country.

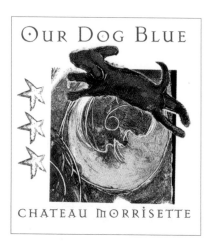

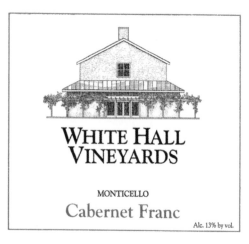

European heritage is strongly felt in Virginia; the Italian wine giant Zonin owns leading Virginia winery Barboursville, and many European winemakers work and consult in the industry, including Michel Rolland. As with its viticulture, the people of the Virginia wine industry are a colorful and diverse group. The well-known rock musician Dave Matthews owns a Blenheim winery near Charlottesville but makes no mention of his name on the bottles, while no fewer than three other Virginia vintners have put representations of themselves on their wine labels.

Vintage Virginia (first weekend in June) and the Virginia Wine Festival (last weekend of September) are two of the oldest and largest wine festivals in the Mid-Atlantic, drawing upward of thirty thousand visitors each weekend, and have played a large role over thirty years in introducing consumers (especially in the suburban Washington, D.C., region) to Virginia wines. Wine-and-food festivals now abound throughout the state, and wineries frequently host events on their properties or jointly with neighboring producers.

—R.L.

(continued)

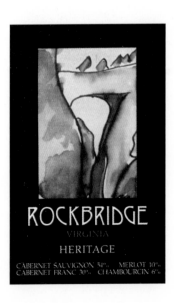

ROCKBRIDGE
VIRGINIA
HERITAGE
CABERNET SAUVIGNON 54%   MERLOT 10%
CABERNET FRANC 30%   CHAMBOURCIN 6%

STATE WEB SITE: www.virginiawines.org

NUMBER OF WINERIES: 101

U.S. RANK FOR NUMBER OF BONDED WINERIES: #5

FIRST WINERY: Farfelu Vineyards, 1967

LARGEST WINERY: Château Morrisette

WELL-KNOWN WINERIES: AmRhein Wine Cellars, Barboursville Vineyards, Blenheim Vineyards, Breaux Vineyards, Cardinal Point Winery, Château Morrisette, Chrysalis Vineyards, Gray Ghost Vineyards, Horton Vineyards, Jefferson Vineyards, King Family Vineyards, Kluge Estate Winery, Linden Vineyards, Rappahannock Cellars, Rockbridge Vineyards, Veritas Vineyard and Winery, Williamsburg Winery, Wintergreen Winery, White Hall Vineyards

Top grapes: Chardonnay, Cabernet Franc, Merlot, Petit Verdot, Viognier, Petit Manseng, Touriga, Vidal Blanc, Chambourcin, Traminette

American viticultural areas: 6—Eastern Shore, Monticello, Northern Neck George Washington Birthplace, North Fork of Roanoke, Rocky Knob, Shenandoah Valley

Wine trails: Bedford Wine Trail, Blue Ridge Wine Way, Blue Ridge Wine Trail, Loudoun Wine Trail, Monticello Wine Trail

Best bets: 2005

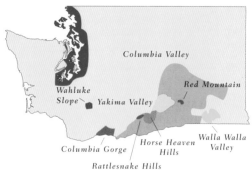

WASHINGTON

As a wine educator, I first mentioned the vineyards and wines of Washington State in the early seventies, a few years after Washington produced its first quality wine. Fast forward forty years, and Washington State has now matured into one of the great wine regions of the world. Today, it is second in the production of wine in the United States after California, but unlike California, Washington State doesn't have a long history of winemaking. It's definitely less about the past and more about the present and the future. Read more about Washington wines and winemaking in Chapter 5.

—K.Z.

State Web site: www.washingtonwine.org

Number of wineries: 323

U.S. rank for number of bonded wineries: #2

First winery: Columbia Winery, 1962

Largest winery: Château Ste. Michelle

(continued)

WELL-KNOWN WINERIES: See Chapter 5

AMERICAN VITICULTURAL AREAS:
9—Columbia Gorge
Columbia Valley
Horse Heaven Hills
Puget Sound
Rattlesnake Hills
Red Mountain
Wahluke Slope
Walla Walla Valley
Yakima Valley

ACRES OF VINES: 30,000 +

U.S. RANK FOR ACRES OF VINES: #3

TOP GRAPES: Merlot, Cabernet Sauvignon, Chardonnay, Syrah, Riesling, Semillon

CAYUSE
VINEYARDS

SYRAH
Cailloux Vineyard
Walla Walla Valley

Alcohol 14.1% by vol.   750 ml

CANOE RIDGE
Vineyard

Merlot
COLUMBIA VALLEY

Alc. 14.0% By Vol.

ESTATE GROWN

RYAN R.C.

L'Ecole N° 41

ALCOHOL 14.4% BY VOLUME

Seven Hills Vineyard • Walla Walla Valley
ESTATE SEMILLON

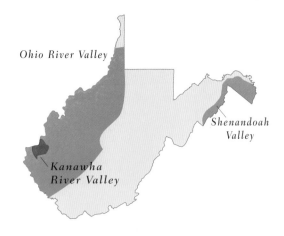

Ohio River Valley

Shenandoah
Valley

Kanawha
River Valley

WEST VIRGINIA

The Mountain State has an abundance of river val-
leys, well-drained soils, and hills in which viticulture
could thrive. However, site selection is crucial as
climate ranges from that of New England on the
Appalachian plateau of Canaan Valley to that of the
Ohio River Valley in the warm southwest. Due to
cold winters and spring frosts, hardy French hybrids
dominate the viticulture, though native varieties
Concord, Delaware, and Norton are also grown
along with Swenson hybrids and Frontenac. Aside
from cold temperatures, other threats to viticulture
include fungal disease, and wildlife depredation
from deer, rodents, birds, and insects.

A few West Virginia wineries grow *vinifera*; Potomac
Highland Winery along the state line in the north
along the Potomac River is the *vinifera* leader, making estate bottled Chardonnay, Riesling, a Meritage
blend, and even a respectable Pinot Noir.

—R.L.

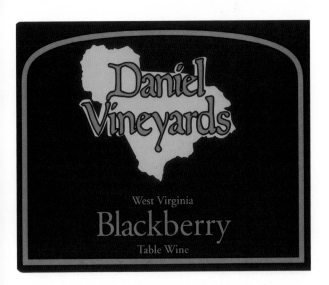

West Virginia

Blackberry

Table Wine

STATE WEB SITE: www.americanwineries.org

NUMBER OF WINERIES: 17

U.S. RANK FOR NUMBER OF BONDED WINERIES: #28

FIRST WINERY: Fisher Ridge Wine Co., 1979

LARGEST WINERY: Daniel Vineyards

WELL-KNOWN WINERIES: Daniel Vineyards, Potomac Highland Winery, Wolf Creek Winery

TOP GRAPES: Seyval Blanc, Vidal Blanc, Cayuga, Chancellor, Chambourcin, Foch, Niagara

AMERICAN VITICULTURAL AREAS: 3—Kanahwa River Valley, Ohio River Valley, Shenandoah Valley

Lake Wisconsin

WISCONSIN

Wisconsin might seem an unlikely place for viticulture. However, those who know the story of Agoston Haraszthy, the flamboyant Hungarian count who founded Buena Vista Winery in Sonoma and with it the modern California wine industry, would be surprised to learn that he had done the same thing previously in Wisconsin. With a talent for site selection, Haraszthy chose a southwestern aspect on a hill above the Wisconsin River near the present town of Prairie du Sac and dug a wine cellar into the hill, still visible today. Prior to his departure to follow the Gold Rush to California, he sold the winery to Peter Kehl, who planted American varieties on the site and produced wine until a deep freeze killed them in 1899.

The Kehl winery, begun in 1857, was revived by Bob Wollersheim in 1973, who planted the cold-hardy Foch variety, now grown by many Wisconsin wineries. While Wollersheim still specializes in Foch-based wines, they diversified into Seyval imported from the Finger Lakes in the mid-1980s, making a hugely successful Prairie Fumé, then added *vinifera* imported from the Columbia Valley. Wollersheim also owns Cedar Creek Winery, which has grown into a successful multigeneration family winery, having bottled its millionth bottle in one production season in 2005.

Wollersheim and other Wisconsin wineries are experimenting with the new generation of cold-hardy hybrids like Frontenac and St. Pepin. Fruit wines are also popular, as are honey-based meads, and due to few acres of native vines and their limited range, many wineries import juice from the West Coast to supplement local fruit and mead products.

—R.L.

STATE WEB SITE: www.wiswine.com

NUMBER OF WINERIES: 24

U.S. RANK FOR NUMBER OF BONDED WINERIES: #23

FIRST WINERY: Kehl Winery, 1857 (now called Wollersheim)

LARGEST WINERY: Wollersheim Winery

WELL-KNOWN WINERIES: Botham Vineyards and Winery, Cedar Creek Winery, Simon Creek Vineyards, Wollersheim Winery

TOP GRAPES: Foch

AMERICAN VITICULTURAL AREA:
1—Lake Wisconsin

Wyoming

Patrick Zimmerer of Table Mountain Vineyards is determined to lift Wyoming out of last place in wine production. He started planting grapes on his family farm in eastern Wyoming in 2001. Since then, he's offered advice and encouragement for his neighbors to try it as well, and they have since formed the Wyoming Grape and Wine Association. Stay tuned.

—S.T.

STATE WEB SITE: www.americanwineries.org

NUMBER OF WINERIES: 3

U.S. RANK FOR NUMBER OF BONDED WINERIES: #49

FIRST WINERY: Terry Ranch Cellars, 1994

WELL-KNOWN WINERIES: Table Mountain Vineyards, Wyoming Craft and Wine Cellars

TOP GRAPES: Frontenac, Frontenac Gris, Maréchal Foch

AMERICAN VITICULTURAL AREAS: none

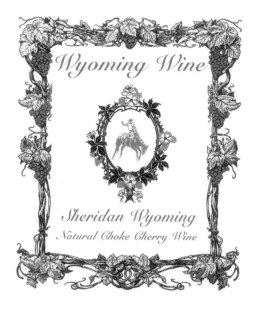

CHAPTER 5

The Major Wine-Producing States

Now that we have looked at the history and overview of American winemaking, let's turn our attention to the four top wine-producing states.

California

No wine-growing area in the world has come so far so quickly as California. Thirty years ago California wines were not necessarily considered worthy of comparison to European wines. Now, California wines are available worldwide, and shipments for export have increased dramatically over recent years to countries including Japan, Germany, and England.

California produces more than 90 percent of U.S. wine. California wines dominate American wine consumption, accounting for about two-thirds of all wine sales in the United States. Wine is also California's most valuable finished agricultural product, accounting for a $45 billion economic impact. If the state of California were a nation, it would be the fourth-leading wine producer in the world!

An Introduction to California Wines

Viticultural Areas

The map on page 78 shows the important wine-making regions you should know. It's easier to remember them if you divide them into five groups:

North Coast: Napa County, Sonoma County, Mendocino County, Lake County (Best wines: Cabernet Sauvignon, Zinfandel, Sauvignon Blanc, Chardonnay, Merlot)

North Central Coast: Monterey County, Santa Clara County, Livermore Valley, Santa Cruz Mountains (Best wines: Syrah, Grenache, Viognier, Marsanne, Roussane, Chardonnay, Pinot Noir)

South Central Coast: San Luis Obispo County, Santa Barbara County (Best wines: Sauvignon Blanc, Chardonnay, Pinot Noir, Syrah)

Sierra Foothills: (Best wines: Zinfandel)

San Joaquin Valley: Known for jug wines

Napa Valley represents about 5 percent of California's wine production.

Acres of wine grapes planted in Napa: 44,771
Number of wineries: 391

Acres of wine grapes planted in Sonoma: 55,877
Number of wineries: 260

Although you may be most familiar with the names Napa and Sonoma, less than 10 percent of all California wine comes from these two regions combined. In fact, the bulk of California wine is produced in the San Joaquin Valley, mostly ordinary table wines, often referred to as jug wines. This region accounts for more than 50 percent of the wine grapes planted. Perhaps that makes California wine seem insignificant—that the production of jug wine dominates California winemaking history—but this is typical of most wine-producing countries. In France, for example, AOC wines account for only 35 percent of all French wines, while the rest are everyday table wines.

Last year, more than 15 million people visited California's wine-growing areas. Vineyards and wineries are the second most popular California tourist destination after Disneyland.

A NOTE ON JUG WINES

The phrase *jug wines* refers to simple, uncomplicated, inexpensive, everyday drinking wine. You're probably familiar with these types of wine: They're sometimes labeled with a generic name, such as Chablis or Burgundy (even though they do not use any of the same grapes as the AOC wines from those regions in France). Inexpensive and well made, these wines were originally bottled in jugs, rather than in conventional wine bottles, hence the name: *jug wine*. They are very popular and account for the largest volume of California wine sold in the United States.

Ernest and Julio Gallo, who began their winery in 1933, are the major producers of jug wine in California. Many people credit the Gallo brothers with converting American drinking habits from spirits to wine. Some other wineries that produce jug wine are Almaden, Paul Masson, and Taylor California Cellars.

I believe the best-made jug wines in the world are from California. They maintain both consistency and quality from year to year.

The Rise of Better Quality Wines

As early as the 1940s, Frank Schoonmaker, an importer and writer, and one of the first American wine experts, convinced some California winery owners to market their best wines using varietal labels (Chardonnay or Cabernet Sauvignon, for example). This was the beginning of the modern California wine industry.

Robert Mondavi is an excellent example of a winemaker who concentrated solely on varietal wine production. In 1966, Mondavi left his family's Charles Krug Winery and started the Robert Mondavi Winery. That major winery was among the first to switch to varietal labeling, which led to higher quality winemaking. "He was able to prove to the public what the people within the industry already knew—that California could produce world-class wines," said veteran winemaker Eric Wente. Mondavi's role was important to the evolution of varietal labeling of California wines.

There are many additional reasons for California's winemaking success, including:

Location: Napa and Sonoma counties, two of the most important regions for quality wine, are both less than a two-hour drive from San Francisco. This proximity encourages both residents and tourists to visit the regions' wineries, most of which offer wine tastings and sell their wines in their own shops.

Weather: Abundant sunshine, warm daytime temperatures, cool evenings, and a long growing season all add up to good conditions for growing many grape varieties. California is certainly subject to sudden changes in weather, but a fickle climate is not a major worry.

The University of California at Davis and Fresno State University: Throughout their history, both schools have been committed to developing outstanding schools of oenology and viticulture. Each has trained many young California winemakers, and their curricula—with their concentration on the scientific study of wine, viticulture, and, most important, technology—have world-class reputations. In fact, early California winemakers sent their children to study oenology at Geisenheim (Germany) or Bordeaux

(France), while today many European winemakers send their children to these California institutions. Their research, focused on soil, different strains of yeast, hybridization, temperature-controlled fermentation, as well as many other viticultural techniques, has revolutionized the wine industry worldwide.

THE 20 TOP-SELLING CALIFORNIA WINES

1. Carlo Rossi (Gallo)
2. Franzia
3. Gallo Label
4. Gallo Reserve Cellars
5. Almaden
6. Inglenook
7. Sutter Home
8. Robert Mondavi
9. Beringer
10. Paul Masson
11. Glen Ellen
12. Vendange
13. Peter Vella
14. Fetzer
15. Sebastiani
16. Kendall-Jackson
17. William Wycliff
18. Taylor California
19. Blossom Hill
20. Turning Leaf (Gallo)

Money and Marketing Strategy: The important role of both money and marketing in the successful launch of any new wine cannot be overemphasized. Marketing may not create the wine, but it certainly helps sell it. As more and more winemakers concentrated on making the best wine they could, American consumers responded with enthusiasm. They were willing to buy—and pay—more as quality improved. To keep up with consumer expectations, winemakers realized that they needed more research, development, and—most important—working capital. The wine industry turned to investors, both corporate and individual.

Since 1967, when the now-defunct National Distillers bought Almaden, multinational corporations have recognized the profit potential of large-scale winemaking and have aggressively entered the wine business. They've brought huge financial resources and expertise in advertising and promotion that have helped assure the success of American wines both domestically and internationally. Other early corporate participants included Pillsbury, Coca-Cola, and even a company from Japan—Otsuka Pharmaceutical Company.

California Wine Style

Style refers to the characteristics of the grapes and of the wine itself, and is the individual winemaker's trademark as an "artist" who tries different techniques to explore the fullest potential of the grapes.

Most winemakers will tell you that 95 percent of winemaking begins with the quality of the grapes. The other 5 percent comes from the "personal touch" of the winemaker. It is also common for winemakers to move around from winery to winery, just as good chefs move from one restaurant to another. They often carry the same "recipe" from place to place, if it is particularly successful, and sometimes they experiment, creating new styles of wine.

Here are just a few of the hundreds of decisions a winemaker must make when developing his or her style of wine:

- When should the grapes be harvested?

- Should the juice be fermented in stainless-steel tanks or oak barrels? How long should it be fermented? At what temperature?

- Should the wine be aged at all? How long? If so,

should it be aged in oak? What kind of oak—American, French?

- What varieties of grape should be blended, and in what proportion?
- How long should the wine be aged in the bottle before it is sold?

And the list goes on. Because there are so many variables in winemaking, producers can create many styles of wine from the same grape variety—so you can choose the style that suits your taste. With the relative freedom of winemaking in the United States, the overall style of all American wines continues to be diverse.

STAINLESS-STEEL FERMENTATION

Stainless-steel tanks are temperature controlled, which allows the winemakers to control the temperature at which the wine ferments. For example, a winemaker could ferment wines at a low temperature to retain fruitiness and delicacy while preventing browning and oxidation.

A 40-YEAR PERSPECTIVE

NUMBER OF BONDED WINERIES IN CALIFORNIA

Year	Wineries
1965	232
1970	240
1975	330
1980	508
1985	712
1990	807
1995	944
2000	1,210
2006	1,600+

Source: *The Wine Institute*

The California Wine Conundrum

The renaissance of the California wine industry began only about forty years ago. Within that short period of time, some fourteen hundred new wineries have been established in California; today California lists more than sixteen hundred. Most of these wineries make more than one wine, in a range of styles and prices. For example, you can get a Cabernet Sauvignon wine ranging from "Two Buck Chuck" at $1.99 to Harlan Estate at more than $500 a bottle. Constant change and experimentation keep California winemaking in a state of innovation.

THINKING ABOUT BUYING A VINEYARD IN CALIFORNIA?

Today, unplanted Napa Valley land costs between $100,000 and $200,000 per acre, requires an additional $20,000 per acre to plant, and will produce no income for three to five years. Add the cost of building a winery, buying equipment, and hiring the winemaker. In 2002, Francis Ford Coppola, owner of Niebaum-Coppola Wine Estate, paid a record price of $350,000 an acre for vineyard land in Napa.

One California wine country joke is this: "How do you make a small fortune in the wine business?" "Start with a large fortune and buy a winery."

California Varietal Wine Prices

You can't always equate quality with price. Some of the excellent varietal wines produced in California are well within the budget of the average consumer, although some varietals (primarily Chardonnay and Cabernet Sauvignon) may be quite expensive.

As in any market, supply and demand determine price. However, new wineries are burdened with high start-up costs, which are often reflected in the prices of their wines. Older, established wineries that have amortized their investments are often

FROM THE CORPORATE LADDER TO THE VINE
Some of the pioneers of the
back-to-the-land movement:

"FARMER"	WINERY	PROFESSION
Robert Travers	Mayacamas	Investment banker
David Stare	Dry Creek	Civil engineer
Tom Jordan	Jordan	Geologist
James Barrett	Chateau Montelena	Attorney
Tom Burgess	Burgess	Air Force pilot
Jess Jackson	Kendall-Jackson	Attorney
Warren Winiarski	Stag's Leap	College professor
Brooks Firestone	Firestone	Take a guess!

more reasonable and able to price their wines according to market forces of supply and demand. Remember, when you're buying California wine, price doesn't always reflect quality.

Choosing a California Wine

One reason California produces such a wide variety of wines is its many different climates. Some wine-growing areas are as cool as Burgundy, Champagne, and the Rhein, while others are as warm as the Rhône Valley, Portugal, and the southern regions of Italy and Spain. If that's not diverse enough, these wine-growing areas have inner districts with "microclimates," or climates within climates. One of the microclimates (which are among the designated AVAs) in Sonoma County, for example, is the Russian River Valley.

To better understand this concept, let's examine the Rudd label.

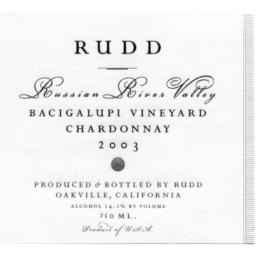

State: California
County: Sonoma
Viticultural Area (AVA): Russian River Valley
Vineyard: Bacigalupi
Winery: Rudd

California wine has no classification system that resembles the European AOC equivalent, but the labels tell you everything you need to know about the wine—and more. Here are some quick tips you can use when you scan the shelves at your favorite retailer. The label shown above will serve as an example.

The most important piece of information on the label is the producer's name. In this case, the producer is Rudd.

If the grape variety is on the label, a minimum of 75 percent of the wine must be derived from that grape variety. The Rudd label shows that the wine is made from the Chardonnay grape.

If the wine bears a vintage date, 95 percent of the grapes must have been harvested that year. This wine label shows that most or all of the grapes were harvested in 2003.

If a wine is labeled with a state or county name, 85 percent of the grapes must come from the vintage year listed on the bottle.

If the wine is designated "California," then 100 percent of the grapes must have been grown in California.

THERE ARE 107 AVAs IN CALIFORNIA. SOME OF THE BEST KNOWN ARE:

Napa Valley

Sonoma Valley

Russian River Valley

Alexander Valley

Dry Creek Valley

Los Carneros

Anderson Valley

Santa Cruz Mountains

Livermore Valley

Paso Robles

Edna Valley

Fiddletown

Stag's Leap

Chalk Hill

Howell Mountain

Sierra Foothills

If the label designates a certain federally recognized viticultural area (AVA), such as Russian River Valley (as on our example), then at least 85 percent of the grapes used to make that wine must have been grown in that location.

If an individual vineyard is noted on the label (Bacigalupa Vineyard, in this case), 95 percent of the grapes must be from that vineyard, which must be located within the approved AVA listed on the label.

The alcohol content is given in percentages. Usually, the higher the percentage of alcohol, the "fuller" the wine will be. This label shows that this wine has 14.1 percent alcohol.

"Produced and bottled by" means that at least 75 percent of the wine was fermented by the winery named on the label.

SOME OF THE FAMOUS INDIVIDUAL VINEYARDS OF CALIFORNIA

Bien Nacido	Gravelly Meadow
Bacigalupa	Martha's Vineyard
Dutton Ranch	McCrea
Durell	S.L.V.
Robert Young	To-Kalon
Bancroft Ranch	Beckstoffer
Geyserville	Monte Rosso

Some wineries tell you the exact varietal content of the wine, and/or the sugar content of the grapes when they were picked, and/or the amount of residual sugar (to let you know how sweet or dry the wine is).

"Reserve" on the label has no legal meaning. In other words, there is no law that defines it. Some wineries, such as Beaulieu Vineyards and Robert Mondavi Winery, still mark some of their wines *Reserve*. BV's Reserve is from a particular vineyard. Mondavi's Reserve is made from a special blend of grapes, presumably their best. Others include Cask wines, Special Selections, or Proprietor's Reserve.

The California Wine Institute has proposed a definition of Reserve to meet the requirement by some export markets.

Winemaking Techniques: California vs. European

European winemaking has established traditions that have remained essentially unchanged for hundreds of years. These practices involve the ways grapes are grown and harvested, and in some cases include winemaking and aging procedures.

In California there are few traditions, and winemakers are able to take full advantage of modern technology. Furthermore, there is freedom to experiment and create new products. Some of the California winemakers' experimentation, such as combining different grape varieties to make new styles of wine, is prohibited by some European wine-control laws. Californians thus have opportunities to try many new ideas—opportunities sometimes forbidden to European winemakers.

Another way in which California winemaking is different from European is that many California wineries carry an entire line of wine. Many of the larger wineries produce more than twenty different labels. In Bordeaux, most châteaux produce only one or two wines.

In addition to modern technology and experimentation, the fundamentals of wine growing can't be ignored: California's rainfall, weather patterns, and soils are very different from those of Europe. The greater abundance of sunshine in California can result in wines with a greater alcohol content, ranging on average from 13.5 percent to 14.5 percent, compared to 12 percent to 13 percent on average in Europe. This higher alcohol content changes the balance, taste, and style of the wines.

Many well-known and highly regarded European winemakers have invested in California vineyards and are making their own wine. There are more than forty-five California wineries owned by European, Canadian, or Japanese companies, as well as many European wineries with operations in California. For example:

- One of the most influential joint ventures matched Baron Philippe de Rothschild, then the owner of Château Mouton-Rothschild in Bordeaux, and Robert Mondavi, of the Napa Valley, to produce a wine called Opus One.
- The owners of Château Pétrus in Bordeaux, the Moueix family, have vineyards in California. Their wine is a Bordeaux-style blend called Dominus.
- Moët & Chandon, which is part of Moët-Hennessy, owns Domaine Chandon in the Napa Valley.
- Roederer has grapes planted in Mendocino County and produces Roederer Estate.
- Mumm produces a sparkling wine, called Mumm Cuvée Napa.
- Taittinger has developed its own sparkling wine called Domaine Carneros.
- The Spanish sparkling-wine house Codorniu owns a winery called Artesa; and Freixenet owns land in Sonoma County and produces a wine called Gloria Ferrer.
- The Torres family of Spain owns a winery called Marimar Torres Estate in Sonoma County.
- Frenchman Robert Skalli (Fortant de France) owns more than six thousand acres in Napa Valley and the winery St. Supery.
- Tuscan wine producer Piero Antinori owns Atlas Peak winery in Napa.

Devastation in the 1980s: The Return of Phylloxera

In the 1980s the plant louse phylloxera destroyed a good part of the vineyards in California, costing a billion dollars in new plantings. Now this may sound strange, but it proved that good can come from bad. So what's the good news?

This time, vineyard owners didn't have to wait to discover a solution; they already knew what they would have to do to replace the dead vines—by replanting with a different rootstock that they knew was resistant to phylloxera. So while the short-term effects were terribly expensive, the long-term result should be better quality wine.

In the early days of California grape growing, little thought was given to where a specific grape would grow best. Chardonnays were planted in climates that were much too warm, and Cabernet Sauvignons were planted in climates that were much too cold.

After the onset of phylloxera, winery owners were forced to rectify their errors and, when replanting, they matched the climate and soil with the appropriate grape variety. Grape growers have also had the opportunity to plant different grape clones. The biggest change was in the planting density of the vines themselves. Traditional spacing used by most wineries before phylloxera was somewhere between four hundred and five hundred vines per acre. Today with the new replanting, it is not uncommon to have more than a thousand vines per acre.

The bottom line is that if you like California wines now, you'll love them more with time. The quality is already better and the costs are lower—a win-win situation for everyone.

The White Wines of California
Chardonnay—The Major White Grape Variety in California

There are more than twenty-four different varieties of white wine grapes grown in California, but the most important is Chardonnay (*Vitis vinifera*). This green-skinned grape is considered by many the finest white grape variety in the world. It is responsible for all the great French white Burgundies, such as Meursault, Chablis, and Puligny-Montrachet. In California, it has been the most successful white grape, yielding a wine of tremendous character and magnificent flavor. More than eight hundred different California Chardonnays are available to the consumer. The wines are often aged in small oak barrels, increasing their complexity. Because of their popularity, the grapes command high prices. Chardonnay is always dry and benefits from aging more than any other American white wine. Superior examples can keep and develop well in the bottle for five years or longer.

The Chardonnay Price Differential
You will find that a number of Chardonnays cost more than other varietals. As mentioned above, many wineries age these wines in wood—sometimes for more than a year. Oak barrels have doubled in price over the last five years, averaging seven hundred dollars per barrel. Add to this the cost of the grapes and the length of time before the wine is actually sold, and you can see why the best of the California Chardonnays cost more than twenty-five dollars per bottle.

Variations in Taste
To explain the variety of different-tasting Chardonnays available, think of this: There are many brands of

ice cream on the market. They use similar ingredients, but there is only one Ben & Jerry's. The same is true for wine. Among the many things to consider:

Is a wine aged in wood or stainless steel?

If wood, what type of oak?

Was there barrel fermentation?

Did the wine undergo a malolactic fermentation (conversion of malic acid to lactic acid in wine)?

How long did the wine remain in the barrel (part of the style of the winemaker)?

Where did the grapes come from?

The aromas associated with Chardonnay have inspired descriptions ranging from apple, grapefruit, citrus, melon, and pineapple to butter, oak, toast, and vanilla.

Malolactic fermentation is a second fermentation that lowers tart malic acids and increases the softer lactic acids, making for a richer style wine. The result is what many wine tasters refer to as a buttery bouquet.

KEVIN ZRALY'S FAVORITE CHARDONNAYS

Acacia	Kongsgaard
Au Bon Climat	Landmark
Arrowood	Marcassin
Beringer	Martinelli
Cakebread	Mer Soleil
Chalk Hill	Peter Michael
Chateau Montelena	Robert Mondavi
Chateau St. Jean	Pahlmeyer
Dutton Goldfield	Phelps
Gary Farrell	Ramey
Ferrari-Carano	Rudd Estate
Flora Springs	Saintsbury
Grgich Hills	Silverado
Hanzell	Talbott
Paul Hobbs	Williams Selyem
Kistler	

CALIFORNIA CHARDONNAY

BEST BETS

1997*
1999*
2000
2001*
2002*
2003*
2004*
2005

*Note: * signifies exceptional vintage*

The two leading white table wines produced in the United States in 2006 were Chardonnay and Sauvignon Blanc/Fumé Blanc.

The Other Major California White Wine Grapes

Sauvignon Blanc

Sometimes labeled Fumé Blanc, this is one of the grapes used in making the dry white wines of the Graves region of Bordeaux and the white wines of Sancerre and Pouilly-Fumé in the Loire Valley of France, as well as in New Zealand. California Sauvignon Blanc makes one of the best dry white wines in the world. It is sometimes aged in small oak barrels and occasionally blended with the Sémillon grape. The aromas of Sauvignon Blanc have been described as grapefruit, grass, herbs, and cat pee.

KEVIN ZRALY'S FAVORITE SAUVIGNON BLANCS

Caymus
Chalk Hill
Chateau St. Jean
Dry Creek
Ferrari-Carano
Grgich Hills
Gainey
Mantanzas Creek
Mason
Robert Mondavi
Phelps
J Rochioli
Silverado
Simi

Why is Sauvignon Blanc often labeled as Fumé Blanc? Robert Mondavi realized that no one was buying Sauvignon Blanc, so he changed its name to Fumé Blanc. Strictly a marketing maneuver—it was still the same wine. Result: Sales took off. To share his success, Mondavi decided not to trademark the name, so now anyone can use it (and many producers do).

Chenin Blanc

This is one of the most widely planted grapes in the Loire Valley of France. In California, the grape yields a very attractive, soft, light-bodied wine. It is usually made very dry or semisweet; it is a perfect apéritif wine, simple and fruity.

Viognier

One of the major white grapes from the Rhône Valley in France, Viognier thrives in warmer and sunny climates, so it's a perfect grape for the weather conditions in certain areas of California. It has a distinct fragrant bouquet. Not as full-bodied as most Chardonnays, nor as light as most Sauvignon Blancs, it's an excellent food wine.

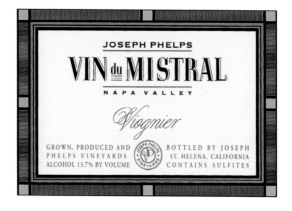

Riesling

Responsible for the best German wines of the Rhein and Mosel and the Alsace wines of France, this grape produces white wines of distinctive varietal character in every style from bone-dry to very sweet dessert wines, which are often much better by themselves than with dessert. The smell of Riesling at its finest is always lively, fragrant, and both fruity and flowery. Until January 2006 it was also labeled as Johannisburg Riesling.

White Wine Trends

There has been a trend toward wineries specializing in particular grape varieties. Twenty years ago, I would have talked about which wineries in California were the best. Today, I'm more likely to talk about which winery, AVA, or individual vineyard makes the best Chardonnay; which winery makes the best Sauvignon Blanc; and the same would hold true for the reds, as you'll see.

The era of great experimentation with winemaking techniques is slowing down, and now the winemakers are making the finest possible wines they can from what they've learned in the 1980s and 1990s. I do expect to see some further experimentation to determine which grape varieties grow best in the various AVAs and microclimates. One of the biggest changes in recent years is that wineries have also become more food-conscious in winemaking, adjusting their wine styles to go better with various kinds of food by adjusting the alcohol, tannin, and acidity.

Chardonnay is the major white wine grape variety planted in California. (Cabernet Sauvignon and Merlot are the major red varieties, with more Syrah being planted.) Sauvignon Blanc (also called Fumé Blanc) wines have greatly improved; they're easier to consume young and while they still don't have the cachet of a Chardonnay, they are now better matched with most foods, I find. However, other white-grape varieties such as Chenin Blanc aren't meeting with the same success, and they're harder to sell. Still, just to keep it interesting, some winemakers are planting more European varietals, such as Viognier.

Another significant development in California winemaking is the extent to which giant corporations have been buying up small, midsize, and even large wineries. The wine industry, like so many other businesses these days, has been subject to a great deal of consolidation as a result of mergers and acquisitions. See the list opposite for some notable examples of this trend.

MERGERS AND ACQUISITIONS:
A WINERY BY ANY OTHER NAME

Here, listed by the parent company, is a selection of some well-known wineries and brands.

ALLIED DOMECQ PLC

Atlas Peak, Buena Vista, Callaway Coastal Vineyards, Clos du Bois, William Hill, Mumm Napa

BERINGER BLASS (FOSTER'S)

Beringer Vineyards, Carmenet, Chateau Souverian, Chateau St. Jean, Etude Wines, Meridian Vineyards, St. Clement, Stags' Leap Winery, Stone Cellars, Windsor

CONSTELLATION BRANDS, INC.

Batavia Wine Cellars, Canandaigua Winery (includes Arbor Mist, J. Roget, Richards, Taylor), Columbia Winery, Covey Run Winery, Dunnewood Vineyards, Estancia Winery, Franciscan Vineyards, Mission Bell Winery (includes Almaden, Cook's Cribari, Inglenook, Le Domaine Paul Masson, Taylor California Cellars), Robert Mondavi Napa, Robert Mondavi Private Selection, Robert Mondavi Winery, Mount Veeder Winery, Opus One, Quintessa, Ravenswood, Simi Winery, Ste. Chapelle Winery, Paul Thomas Winery, Turner Road Vintners (includes Heritage, La Terre, Nathanson Creek, Talus, Vendange)

DIAGEO

Beaulieu Vineyards, Blossom Hill, BV Coastal, The Monterey Vineyard, Painted Hills, Sterling Vineyards

ERNEST AND JULIO GALLO

Anapamu Cellars, Frei Brothers Reserve, Gallo of Sonoma, Indigo Hills, MacMurray Ranch, Marcelina Vineyards, Louis M. Martini, Mirassou Vineyards, Rancho Zabaco, Redwood Creek, Turning Leaf

THE WINE GROUP

Colony, Concannon, Corbett Canyon, Franzia, Glen Ellen, Lejon, Mogen David, Summit, M. G. Vallejo

Source: *Wines & Vines*

MARGRIT BIEVER AND ROBERT MONDAVI:

With Chardonnay: oysters, lobster, a more complex fish with beurre blanc sauce, pheasant salad with truffles. With Sauvignon Blanc: traditional white meat or fish course, sautéed or grilled fish (as long as it isn't an oily fish).

DAVID STARE (DRY CREEK):

With Chardonnay: fresh boiled Dungeness crab cooked in Zatarain's crab boil, a New Orleans–style seasoning. Serve this with melted butter and a large loaf of sourdough French bread. With Sauvignon Blanc, "I like fresh salmon cooked in almost any manner. Personally, I like to take a whole fresh salmon or salmon steaks and cook them over the barbecue in an aluminum foil pocket. Place the salmon, onion slices, lemon slices, copious quantities of fresh dill, salt, and pepper on aluminum foil and make a pocket. Cook over the barbecue until barely done. Place the salmon in the oven to keep it warm while you take the juices from the aluminum pocket, reduce the juices, strain, and whisk in some plain yogurt. Enjoy!"

WARREN WINIARSKI (STAG'S LEAP WINE CELLARS):

With Chardonnay: seviche, shellfish, salmon with a light hollandaise sauce.

JANET TREFETHEN (TREFETHEN VINEYARDS):

With Chardonnay: barbecued whole salmon in a sorrel sauce. With White Riesling: sautéed bay scallops with julienne vegetables.

RICHARD ARROWOOD (ARROWOOD VINEYARDS AND WINERY):

With Chardonnay: Sonoma Coast Dungeness crab right from the crab pot, with fennel butter as a dipping sauce.

BO BARRETT (CHATEAU MONTELENA WINERY):

With Chardonnay: salmon, trout, or abalone, barbecued with olive oil and lemon leaf and slices.

JACK CAKEBREAD (CAKEBREAD CELLARS):

"With my Cakebread Cellars Napa Valley Chardonnay: bruschetta with wild mushrooms, leek and mushroom–stuffed chicken breast, and halibut with caramelized endive and chanterelles."

ED SBRAGIA (BERINGER VINEYARDS):

With Chardonnay: lobster or salmon with lots of butter.

THE RED WINES OF CALIFORNIA

When I first began studying wines in 1970, people were more interested in red wine than white. From the mid-1970s, when I started teaching, into the mid-1990s, my students showed a definite preference for white wine. Fortunately for me (since I am a red-wine drinker), the pendulum is surely swinging back to more red-wine drinkers. The chart below shows you the trend of wine consumption in the United States over the last thirty-five years.

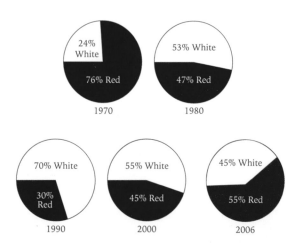

RED VS. WHITE—CONSUMPTION IN THE UNITED STATES

Looking back at the American obsession with health and fitness in the 1970s and 1980s, many people switched from meat and potatoes to fish and vegetables—a lighter diet that called more for white wine than red. "Chardonnay" became the new buzzword that replaced the call for "a glass of white wine." Bars that never used to stock wine—nothing decent, anyway—began to carry an assortment of fine wines by the glass, with Chardonnay, by far, the best-selling wine. Today, steak is back and the new buzzwords are Cabernet Sauvignon and Syrah.

Finally, perhaps the most important reason that red wine consumption has increased in the United States is that California is producing much better quality red wines than ever before. One of the reasons for improved quality is the replanting of vines over the last twenty years as a result of the phylloxera problem. Some analysts thought the replanting would be financially devastating to the California wine industry, but in reality it may have been a blessing in disguise, especially with regard to quality.

The opportunity to replant allowed vineyard owners to increase their red-grape production. It enabled California grape growers to utilize the knowledge they have gained over the years with regard to soil, climate, microclimate, trellising, and other viticultural practices. As a result, from 1991 to 2006, sales of red wine in all of the United States grew by more than 125 percent.

Breaking California's acreage down further:

- In 2006 there were 290,223 acres in red grapes and 180,774 in white grapes planted in California.

- Napa is red wine country, with 27,000-plus acres in red grapes versus 11,000 acres in whites. Leading the red grapes is Cabernet Sauvignon, with 14,000 acres, while Chardonnay is the king of the whites with 9,000 acres.

THE FRENCH PARADOX

In the mid-1990s, the TV series 60 Minutes twice aired a report on a phenomenon known as the French Paradox—the fact that the French have a lower rate of heart disease than Americans, despite a diet that's higher in fat. Since the one thing the American diet lacks, in comparison to the French diet, is red wine, some researchers were looking for a link between the consumption of red wine and a decreased rate of heart disease. Not surprisingly, in the year following this report, Americans increased their purchases of red wines by 39 percent.

The Major Red Grapes in California

While there are more than thirty red grape varieties planted in California, the top five red grapes are Cabernet Sauvignon, Pinot Noir, Zinfandel, Merlot, and Syrah.

Cabernet Sauvignon

Considered the most successful red grape in California, Cabernet Sauvignon yields some of the greatest red wines in the world. Cabernet is the predominant variety used in the finest red Bordeaux wines, such as Château Lafite-Rothschild and Château Latour. Almost all California Cabernets are dry, and depending upon the producer and vintage, they range in style from light and ready to drink to extremely full bodied and long lived. California Cabernet has become the benchmark for some of the best wines in the world.

Aromas that are typically characteristic of Cabernet Sauvignon are blackberry, cassis, black cherry, and eucalyptus. Most Cabernet Sauvignons are blended with other grapes, primarily Merlot. To include the grape variety on the label, however, the winemaker must use at least 75 percent Cabernet Sauvignon.

THE HESS
COLLECTION
MOUNT VEEDER
NAPA VALLEY CABERNET SAUVIGNON
2001

KEVIN ZRALY'S FAVORITE CALIFORNIA CABERNET SAUVIGNONS

Arrowood
Beaulieu Private Reserve
Beringer Private Reserve
Cakebread
Caymus Special Selection
Chateau Montelena
Chateau St. Jean-Cinq/Cepages
Dalla Valle
Diamond Creek
Duckhorn
Dunn Howell Mountain
Gallo of Sonoma Estate
Groth Reserve
Heitz
Hess Collection
Paul Hobbs
Jordan
Joseph Phelps
La Jota
Laurel Glen
Louis Martini
Mondavi Reserve
Opus One
Pine Ridge
Pride Mountain
Ridge Monte Bello
Shafer Hillside Select
Silver Oak
Spottswood
Staglin
Stag's Leap Cask
St. Francis
Whitehall Lane

Best bets for Cabernet Sauvignon (north coast)

1994*
1995*
1996*
1997*
1999*
2000
2001*
2002*
2003*
2004
2005*

*Note: * signifies exceptional vintage*

The 2005 vintage in California was the largest wine-grape crop ever, and a great vintage overall.

Pinot Noir

Known as the "headache" grape because of its fragile quality, Pinot Noir is temperamental, high maintenance, expensive, and difficult to grow and make into wine. The great grape of the Burgundy region of France—responsible for such famous wines as Gevrey-Chambertin, Nuits-St-Georges, and Pommard—is also one of the principal grapes in French Champagne. In California, many years of experimentation in finding the right location to plant Pinot Noir and to perfect the fermentation techniques have elevated some of the Pinot Noirs to the status of great wines. Pinot Noir is usually less tannic than Cabernet and matures more quickly, generally in two to five years. Because of the extra expense involved in growing this grape, the best examples of Pinot Noirs from California may cost more than other varietals.

Southern California—especially the Santa Barbara area, as the characters in *Sideways* could tell you—has become one of the prime locations for Pinot Noir production, with plantings up by more than 200 percent in the past decade. In fact, Pinot Noir sales overall have increased at least 20 percent since the film came out. The Carneros district and Russian River Valley, in the North Coast, are also good places for Pinot Noir because of the cooler climate. Common Pinot Noir aromas are red berries, red cherry, leather, and tobacco for older Pinots.

KEVIN ZRALY'S FAVORITE CALIFORNIA PINOT NOIRS

Acacia
Artesa
Au Bon Climat
Calera
Carneros Creek
Cline
Dehlinger
Merry Edwards
Etude
Gary Farrell
Flowers
Paul Hobbs
Marcassin
Robert Mondavi
Morgan
J. Rochioli
Saintsbury
Sanford
Williams Selyem

One author, trying to sum up the difference between a Pinot Noir and a Cabernet Sauvignon, said, "Pinot is James Joyce, while Cabernet is Dickens. Both sell well, but one is easier to understand."

BEST BETS FOR PINOT NOIR (NORTH COAST)

2002*
2003*
2004*
2005*

Note: * signifies exceptional vintage

Zinfandel

The surprise grape of California, Zinfandel was used to make "generic" or jug wines in the early years of California winemaking. Over the past twenty years, however, it has developed into one of the best red varietal grapes. The only problem in choosing a Zinfandel wine is that so many different styles are made. In the 2005 vintage, Turley winery made eighteen different Zinfandels. Depending on the producer, the wines can range from a big, rich, ripe, high-alcohol, spicy, smoky, concentrated, intensely flavored style with substantial tannin, to a very light, fruity wine. And let's not forget white Zinfandel! Some Zinfandels have more than 16 percent alcohol. Recent DNA studies have concluded that Zinfandel is the same grape as the Primitivo in Italy.

BEST BETS FOR ZINFANDEL (NORTH COAST)

1994*
1995*
1997*
1999*
2001
2002*
2003*
2004
2005*

Note: * signifies exceptional vintage

Carlisle
Cline
Dry Creek
Merry Edwards
Fife
Martinelli
Rafanelli
Ravenswood
Ridge
J. Rochioli
Rosenblum
Roshambo
Seghesio
Signorello
St. Francis
Turley

Merlot

In the early years of California winemaking, Merlot was thought of as a grape only to be blended with Cabernet Sauvignon, because Merlot's tannin is softer and its texture is more supple. It was used to balance the harsh tannins of Cabernet. Merlot has now achieved its own identity as a superpremium varietal. Of red grape varietals in California, Merlot saw the fastest rate of new plantings over the last twenty years. It produces a soft, round wine that generally does not need the same aging as a Cabernet Sauvignon. It is a top seller at restaurants, where its early maturation and compatibility with food make it a frequent choice by consumers.

There were only two acres of Merlot planted in all of California in 1960. Today there are more than fifty thousand!

Common Merlot aromas are blackberry, cassis, cherry, chocolate, coffee, and oak.

Best bets for Merlot (north coast)

2001*
2002*
2003*
2004
2005*

Note: * signifies exceptional vintage

Kevin Zraly's favorite Merlots

Beringer Howell Mountain
Chimney Rock
Clos du Bois
Duckhorn
Franciscan
Havens
Lewis Cellars
Markham
Matanzas Creek
Newton
Phelps
Pine Ridge
Pride
Provenance
Shafer
St. Francis
Truchard
Whitehall Lane

Syrah

The up-and-coming red grape in California is definitely Syrah. I don't know why it's taken so long, since Syrah has always been one of the major grapes of the Rhône Valley in France, making some of the best and most long-lived wines in the world. Further, the sales of Australian Syrah (which they call Shiraz) have been phenomenal in the United States. Americans like the spicy, robust flavor of this grape. It's a perfect grape for California because it thrives in sunny, warm weather.

KEVIN ZRALY'S FAVORITE SYRAHS

Alban
Cakebread
Clos du Bois
Edmunds St. John
Geyser Park
Lewis
Ojai
Fess Parker
Phelps
Qupe
Wild Horse
Zaca Mesa

BEST BETS FOR SYRAH (SOUTH CENTRAL COAST)

2002*
2003*
2004*
2005

*Note: * signifies exceptional vintage*

Red-Grape Boom

Look at the chart below to see how many acres of the major red grapes were planted in California in 1970, and how those numbers have increased. Rapid expansion has been the characteristic of the California wine industry!

TOTAL BEARING ACREAGE OF RED-WINE GRAPES PLANTED— GRAPE-BY-GRAPE COMPARISON

GRAPE	1970	1980	1990	2006
Cabernet Sauvignon	3,200	21,800	24,100	76,756
Merlot	100	2,600	4,000	54,288
Zinfandel	19,200	27,700	28,000	51,425
Pinot Noir	2,100	9,200	8,600	24,442
Syrah			400	18,257

Meritage Wines

Meritage (which rhymes with "heritage") is the name for red and white wines made in America from a blend of the classic Bordeaux wine-grape varieties. This category was created because many winemakers felt stifled by the required minimum amount (75 percent) of a grape that must go into a bottle for it to be named for that variety. Some winemakers knew they could make a better wine with a blend of, say, 60 percent of the major grape and 40 percent secondary grapes. This blending of grapes allows producers of Meritage wines the same freedom that Bordeaux winemakers have in making their wines. For red wine, the varieties include Cabernet Franc, Cabernet Sauvignon, Malbec, Merlot, and Petit Verdot. For white wine, the varieties include Sauvignon Blanc and Sémillon. Some examples of Meritage wines of California:

Cain Five
Dominus (Christian Moueix)
Insignia (Phelps Vineyards)
Magnificat (Franciscan)
Opus One (Mondavi/Rothschild)

OPUS ONE

Opus One was the brainchild of Baron Philippe de Rothschild, proprietor of first-growth Château Mouton Rothschild in Pauillac, Bordeaux, and Robert Mondavi, Napa Valley's creative visionary winemaker. Launched in 1984, Opus One created its own niche as the premiere "ultra-premium" wine. "It isn't Mouton and it isn't Mondavi," said Robert Mondavi. Opus One is a Bordeaux-style blend made from Cabernet Sauvignon, Merlot, and Cabernet Franc grapes grown in Napa Valley. It was originally produced at the Robert Mondavi Winery in Napa Valley but is now produced across Highway 29 in its own spectacular winery.

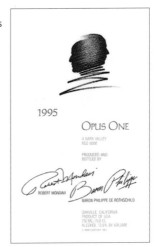

Wine collectors started a frenzy by buying Cabernet Sauvignon from small California wineries at extraordinary prices. These "cult" wineries produce very little wine—with hefty price tags.

Araujo	4,000 cases
Dalla Valle	2,500 cases
Harlan Estate	1,800 cases
Bryant Family	1,000 cases
Screaming Eagle	500 cases
Colgin Cellars	400 cases
Grace Family	48 cases

Wine Styles

When you buy a Cabernet, Zinfandel, Merlot, Pinot Noir, Syrah, or Meritage wine there is no one way to determine which style of that wine you are getting. Style is not indicated on the label. Unless you just happen to be familiar with a particular vineyard's wine, you're stuck with trial-and-error tastings (someone has to do it!). You're one step ahead, though, just by knowing that you'll find drastically different styles from the same grape variety.

With more than 1,600 wineries in California and more than half of them producing red wines, it is virtually impossible to keep up with the ever-changing styles that are being produced. One of the recent improvements in labeling is that more wineries are adding such important information to the back label— when the wine is ready to drink, whether it should be aged, and even suggestions for food pairings.

To avoid any unpleasant surprises, I can't emphasize enough the importance of an educated wine retailer. One of the strongest recommendations I give—especially to a new wine drinker—is to find the right retailer, one who understands wine and your taste.

One of the most memorable tastings I have ever attended in my career was for the fiftieth anniversary of Beaulieu's Private Reserve wine. Over a two-day period, we tasted every vintage from 1936 to 1986 with winemaker André Tchelistcheff. I think everyone who attended the tasting was amazed and awed by how well many of these vintages aged.

Aging California Reds

California reds, especially from the best wineries that produce Cabernet Sauvignon and Zinfandel, age well. I have been fortunate to taste some early examples of Cabernet Sauvignon going back to the 1930s, 1940s, and 1950s, which for the most part were drinking well—some of them outstanding— proving to me the longevity of certain Cabernets. Cabernet Sauvignon and Zinfandel from the best wineries in great vintages will need a minimum of five years before you drink them, and they will get better over the next ten years. That's at least fifteen years of great enjoyment.

However, one of the things I have noticed in the last ten years, not only tasting as many California wines as I have, but also tasting so many European wines, is that California wines seem to be more accessible when young, as opposed to, say, a Bordeaux. I believe this is one of the reasons California wines sell so well in restaurants. I also have found, however, that most California Cabernets do not have the same ability to age over twenty years as do the best wines from Bordeaux.

Red Wine Trends

Red wines from California have traversed much terrain over the last forty or so years. As time has passed there have been notable agricultural, technical, and stylistic developments in the industry. The 1960s were a decade of expansion and development. The 1970s were about growth, especially in terms of the number of wineries that were established in California and the corporations and individuals that became involved. The 1980s and 1990s were the decades of experimentation, in grape growing as well as in winemaking and marketing techniques.

Over the past ten years I have seen winemakers finally get a chance to step back and fine-tune their wines. Today, they are producing wines that have tremendous structure, finesse, and elegance—characteristics that many wines lacked in the early years of the California winemaking renaissance. The benchmark for quality has increased to such a level that the best wineries have gotten better, but more important to the consumer, even everyday wines (under fifteen dollars) are better than ever before.

Though California winemakers have settled down, they have not given up experimentation altogether, if you consider the many new grape varieties coming out of California these days. I expect to see more wines made with grapes such as the Mourvèdre, Grenache, Sangiovese, and especially Syrah continuing the trend toward diversity in California red wines.

Red wines are no longer the sole domain of Napa and Sonoma. Many world-class reds are being produced in the Central Coast regions of California such as Monterey, Santa Barbara, San Luis Obispo, and Santa Clara.

CALIFORNIA WINERIES SELECTED BY *WINE SPECTATOR* FOR THEIR 2006 CALIFORNIA WINE EXPERIENCE

Acacia
Alcina
A. P. Vin
Araujo
Argyle
David Arthur
Au Bon Climat
Aubert
L'Aventure
Bacio Divino
Barnett
Beau Vigne
Beaulieu
Bennett Lane
Bergström
Beringer
Betz
Bond
Brander
David Bruce
Buehler
Buoncristiani
Burgess
Byron
Calera
Carter
Caymus
Chalk Hill
Chalone
Chappellet
Chateau St. Jean
Chateau Souverain
Chehalem
Chimney Rock
Cornerstone
Corté Riva
Cougar Crest
Robert Craig
Crocker & Starr
Cuvaison Estate
Dalla Valle
Darioush
Delectus
Diamond Creek
Dolce

Domaine Alfred
Domaine Carneros
Domaine Chandon
Domaine Serene
Dominus
The Donum Estate
Duckhorn
DuMol
Dunn
Dutton-Goldfield
Merry Edwards
El Molino
Etude
Far Niente
Gary Farrell
Ferrari-Carano
Fisher
Flora Springs
Foley Estate
Robert Foley
Foxer
Franciscan Oakville
Frank Family
Gallo Family
Gemstone
Geyser Peak
Girard
Gloria Ferrer
Goldeneye
Grgich Hills
Groth
Hall
Hanna
Hanzell
Harlan
HdV
Heitz
Hill Climber
Paul Hobbs
Iron Horse
J Vineyards & Winery
JC Cellars
John Anthony
Justin
Keller

(continued)

Kathryn Kennedy
Kenwood
Kistler
Klinker Brick
Kosta Browne
Kunde
Ladera
Lagier Meredith
Lail
Landmark
Lang & Reed
Lewis
Loring
Luna
MacRostie
Margerum
Marimar Estate
Markham
Marston Family
Martinelli
Mer Soleil
Meridian
Merryvale
Peter Michael
Robert Mondavi
Morgan
Mueller
Mumm Napa
Neyers
Nickel & Nickel
Northstar
Novy
Olabisi
Opus One
Pahlmeyer
Paloma
Papapietro Perry
Patz & Hall
Penner-Ash
Peju Province
Joseph Phelps
Pine Ridge
PlumpJack
Pride Mountain
Provenance
Quintessa
Quixote
Qupé
Ramey

Martin Ray
Raymond
Ridge
Roederer Estate
Rosenblum
Stephen Ross
Rubicon Estate
Rutherford Hill
St. Clement
St. Francis
St. Supéry
Sanford
Sbragia Family
Schrader
Schramsberg
Sebastiani
Seghesio
Selene
Sequum
Shafer
Siduri
Silver Oak
W. H. Smith
Snowden
Sonoma-Loeb
Spottswoode
Spring Valley
Stag's Leap Wine Cellars
Staglin Family
Steele
Sterling
Rodney Strong
Tablas Creek
Robert Talbott
Talley
Testarossa
Tor Wines
Treana
Trefethen
Trinchero
Truchard
Turnbull
Viader
Villa Mt. Eden
Vine Cliff
Vision
Whitehall Lane
Williams Selyem
Robert Young

MARGRIT BIEVER AND ROBERT MONDAVI (ROBERT MONDAVI WINERY):

With Cabernet Sauvignon: lamb, or wild game such as grouse and caribou. With Pinot Noir: pork loin, milder game such as domestic pheasant, coq au vin.

TOM JORDAN (JORDAN VINEYARD AND WINERY):

"Roast lamb is wonderful with the flavor and complexity of Cabernet Sauvignon. The wine also pairs nicely with sliced breast of duck, and grilled squab with wild mushrooms. For a cheese course with mature Cabernet, milder cheeses, such as young goat cheeses, St. André and Taleggio, are best so the subtle flavors of the wine can be enjoyed."

MARGARET AND DAN DUCKHORN (DUCKHORN VINEYARDS):

"With a young Merlot, we recommend lamb shanks with crispy polenta, or grilled duck with wild rice in Port sauce. One of our favorites is barbecued leg of lamb with a mild, spicy fruit-based sauce. With older Merlots at the end of the meal, we like to serve cambazzola cheese and warm walnuts."

JANET TREFETHEN (TREFETHEN VINEYARDS):

With Cabernet Sauvignon: prime cut of well-aged grilled beef; also—believe it or not—with chocolate and chocolate-chip cookies. With Pinot Noir: roasted quail stuffed with peeled kiwi fruit in a Madeira sauce. Also with pork tenderloin in a fruity sauce.

PAUL DRAPER (RIDGE VINEYARDS):

With Zinfandel: a well-made risotto of Petaluma duck. With aged Cabernet Sauvignon: Moroccan lamb with figs.

WARREN WINIARSKI (STAG'S LEAP WINE CELLARS):

With Cabernet Sauvignon: lamb or veal with a light sauce.

JOSH JENSEN (CALERA WINE CO.):

"Pinot Noir is so versatile, but I like it best with fowl of all sorts—chicken, turkey, duck, pheasant, and quail, preferably roasted or mesquite grilled. It's also great with fish such as salmon, tuna, and snapper."

RICHARD ARROWOOD (ARROWOOD VINEYARDS AND WINERY):

With Cabernet Sauvignon: Sonoma County spring lamb or lamb chops prepared in a rosemary herb sauce.

DAVID STARE (DRY CREEK VINEYARD):

"My favorite food combination with Zinfandel is marinated, butterflied leg of lamb. Have the butcher butterfly the leg, then place it in a plastic bag. Pour in half a bottle of Dry Creek Zinfandel, a cup of olive oil, six mashed garlic cloves, and salt and pepper to taste. Marinate for several hours or overnight in the refrigerator. Barbecue until medium rare. While the lamb is cooking, take the marinade, reduce it, and whisk in several pats of butter for thickness. Yummy!"

BO BARRETT (CHATEAU MONTELENA WINERY):

With Cabernet Sauvignon: a good rib eye, barbecued with a teriyaki-soy-ginger-sesame marinade, venison or even roast beef prepared with olive oil and tapenade with rosemary, or even lamb. But when it comes to a good Cabernet Sauvignon, Bo is happy to enjoy a glass with "nothing at all—just a good book."

PATRICK CAMPBELL (LAUREL GLEN VINEYARD):

"With Cabernet Sauvignon, try a rich risotto topped with wild mushrooms."

JACK CAKEBREAD (CAKEBREAD CELLARS):

"I enjoy my 1994 Cakebread Cellars Napa Valley Cabernet Sauvignon with farm-raised salmon with a crispy potato crust or an herb-crusted Napa Valley rack of lamb, with mashed potatoes and a red wine sauce."

Ed Sbragia (Beringer Vineyards):

"I like my Cabernet Sauvignon with rack of lamb, beef, or rare duck."

Tom Mackey (St. Francis):

With St. Francis Merlot Sonoma County: Dungeness crab cakes, rack of lamb, pork roast, or tortellini. With St. Francis Merlot Reserve: hearty minestrone or lentil soup, venison, or filet mignon, or even a Caesar salad.

WASHINGTON STATE

In Washington State, the climatic conditions are a little cooler and rainier than in California, but it's neither too cold nor too wet to make great wine in the vineyards. Most of the winegrowing regions are protected from Washington's famous rains by the Cascade Mountains. The earliest record of grape growing in Washington can be traced back to 1825, while the beginning of its modern winemaking industry can be dated to 1967, with the first wine produced under the Chateau Ste. Michelle label.

The four major white grapes grown in Washington State are Chardonnay, Riesling, Gewürztraminer, and Sauvignon Blanc. Washington State has more Riesling planted than any other state in the United States. In the 1960s and 1970s, Washington was known only for white wines, but now it has become known as one of the great American states for the production of red wines, especially Merlot and Cabernet Sauvignon. (As it turns out, the state's Columbia Valley is on the same latitude as Bordeaux, France.) Over the last ten years Washington winemakers have increased their plantings of Syrah and Cabernet Franc, and the recent vintages are turning out to be of very high quality. In 2006, Washington State's wine production was 47 percent red versus 53 percent white.

There are nine AVAs: Columbia Gorge, Columbia Valley, Puget Sound, Red Mountain, Walla Walla, Yakima, Horse Heaven Hills, Wahluke Slope, and Rattlesnake Hills.

AVA (Date AVA established)	Number of Wineries
Yakima (1983)	50
Walla Walla (1984)	110
Columbia Valley* (1984)	100+
Puget Sound (1995)	100
Red Mountain (2001)	12
Columbia Gorge (2004)	15
Horse Heaven Hills (2005)	4
Wahluke Slope (2006)	3
Rattlesnake Hills (2006)	17

* Largest viticultural area, responsible for 95 percent of production.

In 1990 in Washington, there were fewer than 70 wineries, which turned out less than 2 million cases. Today there are more than 400 wineries, producing more than 7.5 million cases of wine. Acreage has increased from 10,000 acres to more than 30,000. Some of the wineries to look for include Betz Family Winery; Canoe Ridge; Cayuse; Chateau Ste. Michelle, Washington's largest winery; Columbia Crest; Columbia Winery; Hogue Cellars; L'Ecole No. 41; Leonetti Cellars; McCrea Cellars; Quilceda Creek; Seven Hills; Andrew Will; and Woodward Canyon Winery.

Chateau Ste. Michelle has formed a winemaking partnership with the famous German wine producer Dr. Loosen. The new Riesling wine is called Eroica.

They have also joined with the Italian wine family Antinori, making a wine called Col Solare.

WASHINGTON BEST BETS

2001*
2002*
2004*
2005

*Note: * signifies exceptional vintage*

VITAL STATISTICS

OREGON

14,100 acres, 303 wineries

WASHINGTON

More than 30,000 acres, 323 wineries

NEW YORK

31,000 acres, 210 wineries

NAPA VALLEY

44,771 acres, 393 wineries

OREGON

Although grapes were planted and wine was made as early as 1847 in Oregon, the modern era began in the early 1960s. Today, Oregon, because of its climate, is becoming well known for Burgundy-style wines. By *Burgundy-style* I'm referring to Chardonnay and Pinot Noir, which are the major grapes planted in Oregon. Many critics feel the best Pinot Noir grown in the United States is from Oregon, with the 2002 vintage being its best ever. Another success in Oregon is Pinot Gris (aka Pinot Grigio), which has recently overtaken Chardonnay as the most widely planted white grape in the state. The largest producer of Pinot Gris (Grigio) in the United States is King Estate in Oregon.

The major AVA in Oregon is the Willamette Valley, near Portland. About 70 percent of Oregon's wineries are located there. Other AVAs include Applegate Valley, Rogue Valley, and Umpqua. Three others, the Columbia Valley, Columbia Gorge, and Walla Walla, are AVAs of both Oregon and Washington State.

OREGON BEST BETS

1999*
2001
2002**
2003
2004*

*Note: * signifies exceptional vintage*
*** one of the best vintages ever for Pinot Noir in Oregon*

Wineries to look for include:

Adelsheim	Eyrie Vineyards
Archery Summit	King Estate
Argyle	Ponzi Vineyards
Beaux Frères	Rex Hill
Bergström	Sokol Blosser
Bethel Heights	Tualatin Estate
Cristom	St. Innocent
Domaine Serene	Ken Wright Cellars
Erath	

Also, the famous Burgundy producer Joseph Drouhin owns a winery in Oregon called Domain Drouhin, producing, not surprisingly, Burgundy-style wines.

NEW YORK STATE

New York is the third largest wine-producing state in the United States, with nine AVAs and more than two hundred wineries. The three premium wine regions are:

Finger Lakes (90 wineries): With the largest wine production east of California, the Finger Lakes region accounts for 85 percent of New York State's wine production. It is one of the greatest wine regions in the world for the production of Riesling. Acres: 10,187 (1,528 *vinifera*).

Hudson Valley (35 wineries): Comprised mostly of premium farm wineries. This is one of America's oldest wine-growing regions: Grapevines were planted by the French Huguenots in the 1600s. It also boasts the oldest active winery in the United States—Brotherhood, which recorded its first vintage in 1839. Acres: 514 (80 *vinifera*).

Long Island (41 wineries): The climate on Long Island has more than two hundred days of sunshine and a long growing season, making it perfect for Merlot and Bordeaux-style wines. Its three AVAs are the Hamptons, Long Island, and the North Fork. The first winery on Long Island was started in 1973 by Alex and Louisa Hargrave. Since 1995, vine-planted acreage on the North Fork has doubled, and production has surpassed 500,000 cases of wine. Acres: 2,240 (2,205 *vinifera*).

Today, more than 120 of the 210 New York State wineries produce *vinifera* wines. Examples of *Vitis vinifera* grapes are Cabernet Sauvignon, Chardonnay, Merlot, Pinot Grigio, Pinot Noir, Riesling, Sauvignon Blanc, and Syrah.

There are three main categories:
Native American (*Vitis labrusca*)
European (*Vitis vinifera*)
French-American (hybrids)

Native American Varieties

The *Vitis labrusca* grapes are very popular among grape growers in New York because they are hardy and can withstand cold winters. Among the most familiar grapes of the *Vitis labrusca* family are Concord, Catawba, and Niagara. Until the last decade, these were the grapes used to make most New York wines. In describing these wines, words such as foxy, grapey, Welch's, and Manischewitz are often used. These words are a sure sign of *Vitis labrusca*.

European Varieties

More than forty years ago, some New York wineries began to experiment with the traditional European (*Vitis vinifera*) grapes. Dr. Konstantin Frank, a Russian viticulturist skilled in cold-climate grape growing, came to the United States and catalyzed efforts to grow *Vitis vinifera* in New York. This was unheard of—and laughed at—back then. Other vintners predicted that he'd fail, that it was impossible to grow *vinifera* in New York's cold and capricious climate.

"What do you mean?" Dr. Frank replied. "I'm from Russia—it's even colder there."

Most people were still skeptical, but Charles Fournier of Gold Seal Vineyards was intrigued enough to give Dr. Frank a chance to prove his theory. Sure enough, Dr. Frank was successful with the *vinifera* and has produced some world-class wines, especially his Riesling and Chardonnay. So have many other New York wineries, thanks to the vision and courage of Dr. Frank and Charles Fournier.

French-American Varieties

Some New York and East Coast winemakers have planted French-American hybrid varieties, which combine European taste characteristics with American vine hardiness to withstand the cold winters in the Northeast. These varieties were originally developed by French viticulturists in the nineteenth century. Seyval Blanc, Vignoles, and Vidal Blanc are the most prominent white wine varieties; Baco Noir and Chancellor are the most common reds.

Trends in New York State Wines

The most significant developments are taking place on Long Island and the Finger Lakes. On Long Island over the last twenty years, the grape-growing acreage has increased from one hundred acres to more than three thousand acres, with more expansion expected.

The predominant use of *Vitis vinifera* varieties allows Long Island wineries to compete more effectively in the world market, and Long Island's longer growing season offers greater potential for red grapes.

The wines of the Finger Lakes continue to get better as the winemakers work with grapes that thrive in the cooler climate, including European varieties such as Chardonnay, Pinot Noir, and especially Riesling, which is clearly the region's "signature wine."

The Millbrook Winery in the Hudson Valley has shown that this region can produce world-class wines—not only white, but red too, from such grapes as Pinot Noir and Cabernet Franc.

Wineries to look for in New York State

The Finger Lakes

Chateau Lafayette Reneau
Fox Run
Dr. Konstantin Frank
Glenora
Standing Stone
Wagner
Herman Weimer

The Hudson Valley

Benmarl
Brotherhood
Clinton Vineyards
Millbrook
Rivendell

Long Island

Bedell
Castello di Borghese (Hargrave)
Channing Daughters
Lenz
Osprey's Dominion
Palmer
Paumanok
Peconic Bay
Pellegrini
Pindar
Raphael
Schneider
Shinn Estate
Wölffer Estate

Kevin Zraly's Best-Value Picks

I TASTE MORE THAN three thousand wines a year, most of them blind tastings, and one of the great joys of wine tasting is the surprise of giving a high rating to an inexpensive wine. Over the years, I have found certain wineries in the United States that consistently produce great wines at great prices.

Here is a list of my picks for "Best-Value American Wines" and my choices for "Under $50 Values." Most of these wines are available at retail outlets throughout the country.

As you will note, nearly all of these wines are produced in California, with the rest from Washington and Oregon.

I have been fortunate, while traveling around the country, to try Valiant Vineyards from South Dakota, Harperfield from Ohio, Gruet from New Mexico, Dos Cabezas from Arizona, Ste. Chapelle from Idaho, Shelton Vineyards from North Carolina, Chaddsford from Pennsylvania, Kluge from Virginia, Fall Creek from Texas, and hundreds of other great American wines that are not from the "big four" states.

I look forward to a time when I can recommend terrific wines from all fifty states, but for now, because of the complexity of state-by-state alcohol regulations, these other wines are simply not available to consumers on any dependable basis. I would love to have included even my own home state of New York in the list below, but alas, the lack of national distribution for even the better New York State wines makes them difficult to find. For now, you either have to visit the winery or purchase them in a restaurant or retail store in the state. With the recent Supreme Court ruling in favor of interstate shipping, I hope that states will soon revise their laws, paving the way for many of these delightful American wines to be shipped from the winery to your home.

BEST VALUES $25 OR LESS

CALIFORNIA

Amberhill Cabernet Sauvignon

Beaulieu Merlot Costal

Benziger Chardonnay, Merlot, or Cabernet Sauvignon

Beringer Chardonnay and Merlot Founders Estate

Buena Vista Sauvigon Blanc

Carmenet Cabernet Sauvignon

Chateau Souverain Chardonnay and Merlot

Chateau St. Jean Chardonnay and Sauvignon Blanc

Cline Cellars Zinfandel

Eschol Cabernet and Chardonnay

Estancia Chardonnay or Cabernet Sauvignon

Ferrari-Carano Fume Blanc

Fetzer Barrel Select Cabernet, Sauvignon, or Zinfandel

Fetzer Sundial Chardonnay and Merlot Eagle Peak

Forest Glen Merlot, Cabernet Sauvignon, or Shiraz

Forest Ville Selections Cabernet or Chardonnay

Frog's Leap Sauvignon Blanc

Gallo of Sonoma Chardonnay, Cabernet Sauvignon, Pinot Noir, and Merlot

Geyser Peak Sauvignon Blanc

Hawk Crest Chardonnay, Cabernet Sauvignon, or Merlot

Kendall-Jackson Chardonnay Vintners Reserve, Syrah, or Cabernet Sauvignon

Laurel Glen Quintana Cabernet Sauvignon

Liberty School Cabernet Sauvignon

Markham Merlot and Sauvignon Blanc

Mason Sauvignon Blanc

Meridian Chardonnay or Cabernet Sauvignon

Robert Mondavi Woodbridge Selections

Monterey Vineyard Cabernet Sauvignon

Napa Ridge Merlot

Ravenswood Zinfandel Napa Valley

R. H. Phillips Cabernet Sauvignon Barrel Cuvee

Ridge Zinfandel (Sonoma)

Rosenblum Zinfandel Vintners Cuvee

Round Hill Chardonnay

St. Francis Merlot

St. Supery Sauvignon Blanc

Saintsbury Chardonnay

Sebastiani Chardonnay Sonoma County

Silverado Sauvignon Blanc

Simi Cabernet Sauvignon

Simi Sauvignon Blanc or Chardonnay

WASHINGTON STATE

Canoe Ridge Merlot

Chateau St. Michelle Riesling Eroica

Columbia Crest Chardonnay, Merlot, Cabernet
  Sauvignon, and Semillon-Chardonnay

Covey Run Fume Blanc, Chardonnay, and Merlot

Hogue Chardonnay Columbia Valley

Hogue Fumé Blanc, Cabernet Sauvignon, or Merlot

The lists in this chapter are by no means comprehensive. These are wines I have retasted each year and found them to be consistently good.

Best Values $25 to $50

California

Cabernet Sauvignon

Artesa

Beaulieu Rutherford

Beringer Knights Valley

Chateau Souverain, Alexander Valley

Clos du Val

Geyser Peak Reserve

The Hess Collection

Jordan

Mondavi

Joseph Phelps

Raymond

Ridge Santa Cruz

Sebastiani, Alexander Valley

Turnbull

Whitehall Lane

Chardonnay

Arrowood

Beringer Private Reserve

Chalone

Cuvaison

Ferrari-Carano

Kendall-Jackson Grand Reserve

Mondavi

Pine Ridge, Carneros

Sonoma-Cutrer

Merlot

Clos du Bois

Frei Brothers

Shafer

PINOT NOIR

Acacia

Au Bon Climat

Byron

Calera

Etude

Mondavi

Morgan

Saintsbury (Carneros)

SPARKLING

Chandon Reserve

Domaine Carneros

Iron Horse

Roederer Estate

SYRAH

Clos du Bois

Justin

Fess Parker

ZINFANDEL

Ridge Geyserville

Rosenblum-Continente

Seghesio Old Vine

OREGON

Argyle Pinot Noir

Willamette Valley Vineyards Pinot Noir

WASHINGTON STATE

Canoe Ridge Chardonnay

Chateau St. Michelle Chardonnay and
    Cabernet Sauvignon

L'Ecole No. 41 Cabernet Sauvignon

Glossary

Acid: One of the four tastes of wine. It is sometimes described as sour, acidic, or tart and can be found on the sides of the tongue and mouth.

Aroma: The smell of the grapes in a wine.

AVA: Abbreviation for American Viticultural Area.

Baco Noir: A red French hybrid grape

Bitter: One of the four tastes found at the back of the tongue and throat.

Botrytis cinerea (boh-TRY-tiss sin-eh-RAY-ah): A mold that forms on the grapes, known also as "noble rot."

Bouquet: The smell of the wine.

Brix (bricks): A scale that measures the sugar level of the unfermented grape juice (must).

Cabernet Franc (cah-burr-NAY frahnk): A red grape planted primarily in California and New York.

Cabernet Sauvignon (cah-burr-NAY so-vee-NYOH): The most important red grape grown in the world, yielding many of the great wines in the United States.

Chambourcin: A red French hybrid grape

Chaptalization: The addition of sugar to the must (fresh grape juice) before fermentation.

Chardonnay (shahr-dun-NAY): The most important and expensive white grape, now grown all over the world; the best white grape of the United States, especially in California and Washington State.

Concord: A red grape used to make some American, primarily Eastern states', wines.

Decanting: The process of pouring wine from its bottle into a carafe to separate the sediment from the wine.

Estate-bottled: Wine that's made, produced, and bottled by the vineyard's owner.

Fermentation: The process by which grape juice is made into wine.

Jug wine: A simple drinking wine from California that is sold in "jug" bottles.

Long-vatted: A term for a wine fermented with the grape skins for a long period of time to acquire a rich red color.

Mechanical harvester: A machine used on flat vineyards. It shakes the vines to harvest the grapes.

Merlot (mehr-LOW): A red grape that produces great wines in California, Washington State, and Long Island.

Méthode Champenoise (may-TUD shahm-pen-WAHZ): The method by which Champagne is made.

Microclimate: A term that refers to an area that has a climate within a climate. While one area may be generally warm, it may contain a cooler microclimate or region.

Must: Grape juice before fermentation.

Norton: A red native American grape variety

Nose: The term used to describe the bouquet and aroma of wine.

Petite Sirah: A red grape grown primarily in California.

Phylloxera (fill-LOCK-seh-rah): A root louse that kills grape vines.

Pinot Gris (PEE-noh GREE): Also known as Pinot Grigio. Grown in California and Oregon.

Pinot Noir (PEE-noh nwahr): Very successful red grape of California and Oregon.

Reserve: A term sometimes found on American wine labels. Although it has no legal significance, it usually indicates a better quality wine.

Residual sugar: An indication of how dry or sweet a wine is.

Riesling: A white grape grown in the cooler climates of Washington State and New York.

Sauvignon Blanc (SOH-veen-yown blahnk): A white grape grown primarily in Washington State and California (where the wine is sometimes called Fumé Blanc).

Seyval Blanc: A white French hybrid grape

Short-vatted: A term for a wine fermented with the grape skins for only a short time.

Sommelier (so-mel-YAY): The French term for cellar master, or wine steward.

Stainless-steel tank: A container that (because of its ability to control temperature) is used to ferment and age some wines.

Sulfur dioxide: A natural substance used in winemaking and grape growing as a preservative, an antioxidant, and also as a sterilizing agent.

Syrah (see-RAH): A red grape grown primarily in California.

Tannin: A natural compound and preservative that comes from the skins, stems, and pips of the grapes and also from the wood in which wine is aged.

Traminette: A white French hybrid grape

Varietal wine: A wine that is labeled with the predominant grape used to produce the wine, i.e., a wine made from Chardonnay grapes (at least 75 percent) would be labeled "Chardonnay."

Viognier (Vee-own-YAY): A white grape grown primarily in California.

Vitis labrusca (VEE-tiss la-BREW-skah): A native grape species in America.

Vitis vinifera (VEE-tiss vih-NIFF-er-ah): The European grape species used to make both European and California wine.

Zinfandel (zin-fan-DELL): A red grape grown in California.

Index

Photo Credits

Image on page ii © Photo 24/Getty Images.
Image on page iii © Image Source/Getty Images.
Image on page vi © Beth Dixson/Veer.
Image on pages viii–ix © Gerald French/Corbis.
Images on pages x & 6 © Food collection/Getty Images.
Image on page 8 © Craig Aurness/Corbis.
Image on page 11 © Peter Ginter/Getty Images.
Image on page 13 © Jerry Alexander/Getty Images.
Image on page 16 © Peter Ginter/Getty Images.
Image on page 27 © Don Tremain/Getty Images.
Image on page 28 © Photodisc Photography/Veer.
Image on page 32 © JupiterImages/Comstock.
Image on page 44 © Photo 24/Getty Images.
Image on page 46 © Stockbyte/Getty Images.
Image on pages 50 & 73 © Stockbyte/Getty Images.
Image on page 52 © PhotoLink/Getty Images.
Image on page 53 © Andrew Weller/Shutterpoint.
Image on page 54 © Stockbyte.
Image on page 55 © Isabelle Rozenbaum/Getty Images.
Image on page 61 © Stockbyte/Getty Images
Image on page 64 © Gildo Nicolo Spadoni/Veer.
Image on page 68 © Jodie Coston/Acclaim.
Image on page 69 © Stockbyte/Getty Images.
Image on page 70 © Thomas Barwick/Getty Images.
Image on pages 74 & 157 © Peter Ginter/Getty Images.
Image on page 158 © Charles O'Rear/Corbis.
Image on page 176 © Image Source/Getty Images.
Image on page 181 © Charles O'Rear/Corbis.
Image on page 182 © JupiterImages/Comstock.
Image on page 185 © Mitch Hrdlicka/Getty Images.
Image on page 193 © Photo Alto Photography/Veer.
Image on page 195 © Royalty-free/Corbis.
Image on page 204 © Food collection/Getty Images.
Image on page 207 © Grafton Marshall Smith/Corbis.
Image on page 209 © Jerry Alexander/Getty Images.
Image on page 214 © Rita Maas/Getty Images.